AF248712

A HANDBOOK FOR
CONFLICT RESOLUTION IN SOUTH ASIA

A HANDBOOK FOR
CONFLICT RESOLUTION
IN SOUTH ASIA

SUNDEEP WASLEKAR

under the auspices of
FRIEDRICH EBERT STIFTUNG, New Delhi

KONARK PUBLISHERS PVT LTD

KONARK PUBLISHERS PVT LTD
A-149, Main Vikas Marg, Delhi 110092 (India)

A Project of
Parliamentarians for Global Action, New York

With support from
Ford Foundation, New Delhi
Shree Bhikshu Foundation, Bombay
United States Institute of Peace, Washington, D.C.
Winston Foundation, Washington, D.C.

Special thanks to
International Centre for Peace Initiatives, Bombay

Typeset by Dexter Services, Delhi and printed at
Rashtra Rachna Printers, Delhi

Introduction

SINCE the early 1990s, two developments have occurred in South Asia. One, in all the countries of the region which form the South Asian Association for Regional Cooperation, except Bhutan, democratic revival has taken place. Two, the policy community in the region has shown a growing appreciation of the conflict resolution discipline.

This handbook is prepared for the benefit of people's representatives in South Asia giving the background of democratic revival in the region. It assumes that in a democratic system people's representatives have a role to play in resolving conflicts between countries. The handbook intends to contribute to their capacity to do so.

The handbook is aimed at those political leaders who wish to participate in the conflict resolution process. It takes it for granted that there is a political will to resolve conflicts. It is not relevant for those who believe that they can enforce solutions to end conflicts on their own terms. In many conflict situations, there is absence of political will to resolve them; and the greatest challenge is to generate such a political will. But once the political will is generated, how can the participants go about resolving a conflict? The handbook aims at providing a few tips to those who may have the political will but not the knowhow.

Who Should Use this Handbook?

Negotiators and mediators involved or desiring to be involved in political exercises to resolve conflicts should find this handbook useful.

Research and action centres planning to intervene in conflict resolution processes should find the handbook particularly useful.

Funding agencies interested in supporting conflict resolution activities can get an idea from this handbook of how conflict resolution capacity can be developed and what kind of realistic expectations be held from peace projects.

How to Use this Handbook?

The handbook is divided into two parts. Part I concentrates on the process of conflict resolution. Part II deals with conflict situations and peace-making efforts in South Asia.

Chapter 1 explains basic concepts. Terms such as conflict management, conflict resolution, conflict settlement are sometimes vaguely used while each term has a distinct meaning. This handbook is for conflict resolution—not for conflict management or conflict settlement or conflict prevention. It may be useful to some extent for conflict settlement and conflict prevention. It is necessary to understand the difference between various terms and define political objectives clearly in a particular situation.

Chapter 2 explains 'negotiation' and 'mediation'—the two terms most frequently used in a conflict resolution process. It gives tips for those who wish to acquire skills in these two functions. Negotiating for peace or resolving conflicts is different from negotiating in any other situation. Here the objective is to reach a situation acceptable to all the parties to a dispute. Once basic terms are understood from the first chapter and the objectives are clearly defined, the second chapter is necessary reading to make oneself familiar with the approaches, skills and techniques required for pro-peace processes.

Chapter 3 explains the concept of a Conflict Resolution Workshop. This handbook is essentially aimed at suggesting a few 'how to do' ideas for conflict resolution in the non-governmental sector. Conflict resolution by governments takes place through official talks and various political initiatives. Conflict resolution by non-governmental institutions is facilitated at specialized workshops.

Chapter 4 provides a report on the Maldives workshop organized by Parliamentarians for Global Action, the International Centre for Peace Initiatives and the International Peace Academy in 1995. There are different kinds of conflict resolution workshops. Some are 'introductory' type aimed at introducing basic concepts, techniques and skills. Some are 'substantive' meant to produce political results or prepare for official dialogue or influence public policy options. The Maldives workshop was introductory. The chapter begins with organizational lessons drawn from the experience of organizing it. It may be useful for those who want to organize similar workshops. The previous chapter has a model agenda for those who want to organize substantive workshops.

Chapters 5 to 7 are based on the Maldives workshop. They can be used with suitable modifications. Chapter 5 provides illustration of inaugural statements which are essential to set the tone and direction of a workshop. Chapter 6 presents simulation exercises presented at the Maldives workshop. Simulations are necessary in a workshop to create participatory dynamics. They have to be conducted by professional experts. The examples given in this chapter may not be necessarily applicable but experts can draft simulations which would be most relevant for the workshop objectives. Chapter 7 presents a few case studies of conflict resolution. They are useful to distill lessons. Many other case studies can be prepared depending on the focus of the workshop.

Chapters 8 to 10 provide information on conflicts and peacemaking efforts in South Asia. Chapter 8 lists conflicts in the region—including those which are resolved and which are yet to be resolved. Chapter 9 lists conflict resolution projects of non-governmental organizations in the 1990s. Chapter 10 is a proposal for a non-legislative South Asian Parliament prepared by Mr Javed Jabbar, former federal minister of Pakistan, in 1992. He has presented it at several regional fora including the Maldives workshop. Since it is an institution which may provide an innovative mechanism for conflict resolution for political leaders in the region, if it comes into being, it needs to be brought to the attention of those who are thinking about conflict resolution in South Asia.

Acknowledgements

A major part of this handbook is based on a conflict resolution workshop jointly organized by Parliamentarians for Global Action, the International Peace Academy and the International Centre for Peace Initiatives in the Maldives from May 19 to 23, 1995. It was co-hosted by the Citizens' Majlis of the Maldives. Dr Jean Krasno and Mr William Weisberg, with the author, prepared the substantive input of the workshop. Mr Weisberg and Dr Krasno should be particularly credited for providing input on negotiation and mediation and for drafting the simulation exercises.

Contents

PART I

CONFLICT RESOLUTION PROCESS

1
Basic Concepts

CONFLICT Resolution is a new subject. It has emerged as an independent discipline since the 1980s. Conflict itself is an old phenomenon, perhaps as old as human history. But conflict resolution as a scientific method of understanding and resolving conflicts between ethnic identities, religions, classes and nations is new.

For centuries conflicts have been studied as a part of 'strategic studies' or 'international relations'. These two disciplines perceive conflicts from the viewpoint of the protagonist state. They assume that conflict is inherent in human nature and hence inevitable. The natural policy response is acquisition of capability (economic, diplomatic, military hardware).

Since the 1950s conflicts are also studied as part of 'peace research' where conflict is perceived to be a result of incompatible interests. The policy response is provided in terms of a change in the balance of power or a regime change.

Whereas the former tends to be a top-down approach, the latter tends to be a bottom-up approach. In either case, there is an element of partisanism.

Conflict resolution is non-partisan. It assumes that conflict is endemic and solution is possible by scientific exploration of the interests of parties to a dispute and encouraging or facilitating communication between the parties.

Settlement and Resolution

Conflict resolution should not be confused with conflict management which can take different forms such as

—conflict management
—conflict settlement
—conflict resolution
—conflict prevention

Conflict management involves controlling violent eruption of a conflict, imposing, if necessary, an unilateral solution by the stronger party.

Conflict settlement involves formulating a short-term solution to a problem at the risk of its recurrence in the future.

Conflict resolution involves resolving a conflict to the satisfaction of all the parties to the dispute.

Conflict prevention involves identifying a conflict situation and resolving it before it is converted into a full-fledged conflict.

Thus, conflict resolution and prevention are inter-linked.

Conflict Phases

Conflict goes through several phases

—Dispute or disagreement
—Tension or exchange of threats of aggression (either direct or subtle threats)
—War or hostilities during which military force is used
—Post-hostility disputes which are over specific aspects of settlement arising from the war
—Termination in which the dispute is resolved or is no longer the concern of the conflicting parties.

The resolution of conflict can take place at any of the above phases.

The most critical element in conflict resolution is for the parties to want the resolution. If policy-makers do not believe that they can achieve by unilateral action what they want, they look for alternatives. At this stage there is scope for conflict resolution.

Determining the right time for conflict resolution is the most challenging task. The search for the ripe moment leads to the escalation of conflict with cost implications for conflicting parties. When costs are unbearable for both the parties, they are ready to seek resolution of the conflict.

Mr Harold Saunders observes in *The Other Walls* "In many cases, developing the commitment to negotiate is the most complex part of the peace process (conflict resolution) because it involves a series of interrelated judgements. Before leaders will negotiate, they have to judge (1) whether or not a negotiated solution would be better than continuing the present situation (2) whether a fair settlement could be fashioned that would be politically manageable (3) whether leaders on the other side could accept the settlement and survive politically and (4) whether the balance of forces would permit an agreement on such a settlement. In more colloquial language, leaders ask themselves: How much longer can this present situation go on? Is there another way and could I live with it politically?"

Stages in Conflict Resolution
The resolution of conflict passes through the following phases
—Sensing the problem
—Defining the problem
—Judging the present situation (unilateral action or resolution)
—Developing commitment to resolution
—Selecting the process of resolution
  • Direct negotiation
  • Facilitated negotiation
  • Third party mediation
—Preparing for the resolution exercise
—Arranging the resolution
  • Stating the problem
  • Developing options
  • Reaching agreement
—Implementing the agreement

Track Two Diplomacy
An important ingredient in the process of conflict resolution is

track two diplomacy. Traditionally diplomacy has been the prerogative of the government representatives alone. Now, three types of diplomacy is conducted.

—Diplomacy (track one)

(traditional conduct of relations by official government representatives)

—People to people contacts/citizen diplomacy

(Exchange of visits, information, gifts by well meaning citizens from countries in dispute at the grass-root level which normally do not have an impact on state policy) e.g.

- cultural events
- academic seminars and conferences
- citizen exchanges
- youth conventions and camps
- festivals
- educational tours
- etc

—Track two diplomacy

(dialogue between persons from disputing polities, with or without facilitators/mediators, on critical issues where participants have access to their governments and/or ability to influence public opinion) e.g.

- former civil servants, diplomats, military officers
- informal advisers to governments
- members of parliament and political parties

Thus, conflict resolution is conducted at two levels: official initiatives involving state parties and track two diplomacy involving persons having credibility with state parties. Track two diplomacy must be conceptually separated from well-meaning communication between citizen groups. People-to-people contacts create goodwill but they do not contribute directly to conflict resolution between state parties. The critical element in conflict resolution is the possible impact an exercise could have on the state policy. Track two diplomacy involves communication between non-officials who have a place in the political system. Many a time it serves as preparatory process for the substantive political process.

Track two diplomacy is conducted in the form of conflict resolution workshops. There are different types of workshops:
  —Introductory (to introduce conflict resolution concepts, skills and techniques)
  —Substantive (to discuss critical issues)
  —Continuing (to discuss issues, assess them in the larger political process and re-enter on a regular basis)
The workshop organized by the International Centre for Peace Initiatives and Parliamentarians for Global Action in the Maldives in May 1995 was 'introductory'.

The Maldives workshop recommended a regular, unconditional, uninterrupted dialogue between official representatives of five major parties each from India and Pakistan. When the first session of this dialogue takes place in 1996 it will be a substantive workshop.

If the dialogue continues on a regular basis, it will be a continuing workshop.

Those interested in participating in conflict resolution need to know about
  —negotiation and mediation
  —conflict resolution workshop
  —facts and perspectives on conflicts under consideration (including efforts made for resolving such conflicts).

2

Negotiation and Mediation

THERE are two methods of modern conflict resolution: negotiation and mediation. This chapter provides a few tips for negotiators and mediators. These are useful in a conflict resolution workshop as also in a real political exercise. They are meant to help the participants in a conflict resolution process to be prepared for certain do's and don'ts.

Negotiations are directly conducted by the parties to a dispute. Mediation is facilitated by a third party. The former part of this chapter focuses on negotiation and difficulties in negotiation. The latter part discusses mediation.

Negotiating for peace or conflict resolution is different from negotiating for trade, transit, cultural or communication matters. Negotiating for peace is not dictating in the spirit of 'take it or leave it'. It is trying to reach resolution of conflict so that one party does not feel a sense of defeat. The following steps are involved in negotiating for peace.

Step 1. Preparation
    - know your goal
    - internal consultations

Step 2. Define your interest

Step 3. Distinguish between positions and interests

Step 4. Consider the other side's choice/consequences for
    - the ruler himself
    - the ruler's supporters

- the ruler's country (people)

Step 5. Compare current choice with future choices for both parties

Step 6. Generate fresh ideas

Step 7. Accept face-saving for the other side; help the other side project a victory while your own goals are accomplished.

Guidelines for Negotiators

—do not act arrogantly
—do not show contempt
—do not resort to threats immediately
—do not take a hostile attitude
—do not give in to fits of rage
—do not show off
—think clearly before you speak
—keep your feelings hidden
—do not exhibit manipulating skills
—use flattery
—identify the weaknesses of the other side
—become acquainted with the drives and passions of opponents
—be sincere
—learn to look through the masks of others
—distinguish role behaviour from the person

Tactics for Negotiating for Peace

(How to protect your interests and achieve peace)
—have facts and expertise
—explore the other side
—intensify relationship with the other side
—power of persuasion
—strengthening the starting position with knowledge of relevant facts, support of allies, achieving status
—broadening the field of negotiation in the eventuality of a deadlock

Integrative Bargaining

There are different types of approaches to negotiations. The approach which is aimed at solely protecting one's own interests in 'strategic'. The approach which is aimed at finding sustainable solution to a conflict is 'integrative'. It implies being considerate to the perspectives of all concerned parties.

If attempting to find an integrative solution:
- Consider yours and others' options and opportunity costs
- Frame issues in terms of interests, not positions
- Define your interests
- Elicit the other parties' interests
- Acknowledge other parties' perspective
- Seek "objective" standards
- Engage in joint problem solving

The 'joint problem solving' would involve the following:
- Identify key stake holders.
- Attend to internal consensus
  - Begin internal processes prior to negotiations
  - Construct a rationale
  - Consider how to overcome other parties' constituent constraints
- Build multi-party coalitions
  - Invite a third party?

Obstacles in Negotiations

There are different kinds of obstacles in negotiation. They are applicable to the personal environment as also to inter-state disputes. Mr William Weisberg described some of the obstacles to negotiation at the Maldives workshop with the following examples.

1. Principled *vs* Conventional "Strategic" Behaviour

If we approach conflict at the level of interests and share this information with our adversary, we can get what we want.

Is this always the case?

There is the story of one who has 10 oranges and another who has 10 apples.

I have 10 apples, but only eat oranges. The other person has 10 oranges and likes both oranges and apples equally. If we share information, we can trade so that each gets 10 fruits he likes to eat.

But, what if the other person who has 10 oranges is approaching this situation strategically? If I tell this other strategic person that I only eat oranges—and he knows that I value oranges more— he might take advantage of this information and offer to give me only 5 oranges for all 10 of my apples. So, should I share the information on my actual preferences or not?

The Tension: Sharing information about our interests can bring about a more efficient, integrative solution. On the other hand, being more strategic can sometimes help avoid dealing honestly with a scorpion.

Perhaps sometimes it is best to share but we must assess the environment (the other parties' intentions).

2. Cognitive Barriers

Sometimes there are cognitive barriers to agreement.

Suppose you and a friend or spouse are going out to a concert and dinner. When you leave your house, you think that you have two tickets with you and an amount of cash, equal to the cost of the tickets, to spend on dinner. When you arrive at the concert, you discover that you have left the cash at home. What would you do?

On the other hand, what if you discovered that you had the cash and had forgotten the tickets? In either case, you still have the option to go to dinner or the concert. You could sell the tickets for dinner money or you could use the cash to buy new tickets.

Most people, according to research, would decide to go to dinner if they had left the tickets behind and would go to the concert if they had left the cash behind. Both options are available in either scenario, but people are influenced by the framing of the situation. Tickets suggest concert; cash suggests dinner.

Cognitively, the set-up of the situation steers your mind towards one decision pathway. This is important in resolving conflict because it demonstrates the importance of the reference point. And the reference point can change. Let's look at another type of situation.

In Sri Lanka, the Government, and the LTTE in the North and East have been at war over, at least in part, the control of territory. A Federal plan has been difficult, over the years, to sell to either side because it appears to be a concession to both. For the Tigers, who have de facto control of the North, most Federal plans would mean ceding some control of Jaffna. For the Government, which has considered itself in legitimate control of the whole island, any devolution of power in addition to what is already in the constitution, is considered a concession. A Federal plan has been framed as loss to both. People are cognitively, psychologically, averse to loss. This can present a challenge to possibly re-frame the issues under contention to attempt to move away from a framing that highlights the need for major concessions on both sides.

3. Other Psychological Barriers

What would you do if an expert hired you to assist in a negotiation suggested an agreement package that required some concessions, but that satisfied some of your objectives? How would you react?

What if this same package came, not from your expert, but from your adversary?

According to research on reactive devaluation, you would be more likely to reject the package from your adversary simply because it came from the other side. The package is the same, only the source is different.

There are some sound reasons why this might be. In your experience, what might cause this? (If they want it, I might be able to get more; if they want it there must be some way they are trying to take advantage of me . . .)

The tendency to reject a package recommended by our opponent is related to our great impulse to bring our thoughts into balance. This is a phenomenon referred to as the need for cognitive consistency. If we have two seemingly contradictory notions, we attempt to reconcile them.

In Sri Lanka, during the recent cessation of hostilities, people would point to the other side and say "the government just increased the defence budget, they are still planning to use the military option," or "the Tigers are still recruiting in the East, they are not serious about negotiations." Now, both are possibly true, but these are not necessarily accurate assumptions.

When people attempt to simplify reality into dichotomous dimensions (they are for negotiations or are preparing militarily), they are attempting to maintain cognitive consistency. Is this action consistent with a 'yes' or 'no' answer to the dichotomous question I have framed in my mind (are they ready to negotiate)?

Let us suppose, for a moment, that both sides have continued to prepare militarily while being engaged in negotiations, as was the case at some stages in the Sri Lankan conflict. How can we read this?

People tend to read an ambiguous situation in a way that is consistent with their prior attitudes. An enemy who rearms while at the peace table is clearly not serious about negotiations. When looking at a situation that offers contradictions (being at the peace table and also re-arming), we emphasize the aspect of reality that is consistent with our preconceptions. This is referred to as selective perception. Selectivity mechanisms allow us to maintain cognitive consistency. This makes our beliefs resistant to disconfirmation. Beliefs that are resistant to disconfirmation create barriers to resolution of conflict.

Once mistrust is established in the perception of one party, it is very difficult to respond in kind when the adversary sends out a signal of possible cooperation.

One final psychological barrier is self-fulfilling prophesies or how hostile beliefs can actually induce hostile behaviour in others. During the cold war, the US thought that the Soviet Union was building up arms for aggressive purposes, and that the US was responding for defensive purposes. The USSR thought the same. This creates the behaviour in the other no different from what one expects, and traps both parties in a cycle of escalation.

Overcoming Barriers with the Use of Third Parties

Strategic barriers to information-sharing can be avoided through the use of a third party. Negotiators might be more likely to trust a third party with knowledge of their underlying interests. If I tell the third party that I only eat oranges, with a promise by the third party not to share this information until he or she knows what the other party prefers, it can be a good use of an honest broker.

A third party can also work to re-frame the reference point, to move the parties' perceptions away from losses to the gains. Most successful negotiations contain some elements of loss and some of gain.

If the third party can identify underlying interests and differences in value placed upon various issues by each party, gains can also be created to move the focus away from losses. A party might be convinced that somewhat less autonomous control of an area that is not under constant military threat is a gain over greater autonomy under military threat.

Finally, all of the psychological mechanisms associated with the pressure toward cognitive consistency can be addressed by a skilled third party.

Third parties can stress the possibility that everything is not reducible to a yes/no question and answer. The US and USSR might not have been committed to being aggressive or defensive, but might have been induced to be either one. It is not so simple that Israelis and Palestinians are committed to killing each other or to living together, but that events might dictate that they will do one or the other.

Going Beyond Interests to Needs

There is a particular type of interest that is at the core of some conflicts. When we speak of interests, we tend to think of concrete items, such as water, land, or financial resources. But underlying most conflicts are some very basic human needs. Examples of these that have been described by human needs theorists include:

- Physical survival (food, clothing, shelter)
- Security (physical and psychological)
- Community and belonging
- Identity
- Self-determination/autonomy

Disputing parties should ask themselves if the conflict is about interests or needs.

Third Party Mediation

Third party mediation is increasingly popular but it does continue to be resisted by some states. Normally the weaker of the two parties to a dispute desires third party mediation and the stronger one resists it.

In the official political process the third party may be
—a strong state
—United Nations
—a regional organization
—international financial agency (e.g. World Bank)
—a neutral state close to the location of dispute
In track two diplomacy the third party may be
—scholars or practitioners

Barriers to Mediation

—Political costs
  - increasing the profile of the conflict
  - damage to prestige of the government
  - subtle commitment to an unpredictable process
  - accepting forum where concessions may be demanded
—Fear of the role of intermediary
  - fear of introduction of inconvenient ideas
  - fear of unpalatable solution being imposed
  - fear of bad publicity outside conflict zone
  - fear of both parties losing to the benefit of the third party

- risks of incompetence

(The intermediary may not be simply competent and hence mess up the situation and waste the time of the two parties.)

Guidelines for Mediators

—Mediate only if all parties accept the principle of mediation and the particular mediator
—Establish legitimacy
—Make role transparent and clear to the parties (lay down and explain process ground rules at the outset)
—Carefully determine the profile (whether high profile or low profile)
—Respect confidentiality
—Be impartial and neutral
—Have no personal agenda
—Provide total confidence and trust to all parties to the dispute
—Be transparent
—Do not distort communication between parties to the dispute
—Be patient and persistent
—Be backed by some authority
   (powerful state, economic power, resolution of the UN Security Council, etc)
—Be capable of
   - analyzing a problem
   - uncovering hidden interests of parties involved in the conflict
   - identifying commonality
   - generating innovative options for parties to the dispute
   - assessing options and reshaping them if necessary.

Tasks for Mediators

—Explore alternative means to peace/cooperation
—Explore interests of parties/distinguish them from positions
—Facilitate mutual understanding of interests without commitment

—Focus on developing options that reconcile interests
—Suggest procedural 'way out' and 'face savers'
—Organize informal, unofficial brainstorming sessions outside the official process
—Listen to the grievances of the parties with seriousness
—Help develop confidence-building measures
—Encourage parties to attack problem rather than each other
—Encourage parties to address each other rather than constituencies back home.

3

Conflict Resolution Workshop

ONE of the most recent innovations in track two diplomacy is the concept of a Conflict Resolution Workshop. Pioneered by Dr John Burton, it was developed by Dr Herbert Kelman of Harvard, International Peace Academy, UN Institute for Training and Research, and others.

A Conflict Resolution Workshop brings together representatives of parties to the dispute in a controlled environment. It is facilitated by trained professionals who have knowledge of conflict theories and experience in team work. The antagonists interact with each other for a few days in close quarters to address conflicts between their polities. They come to the workshop with an intention to understand each other and search solutions to their conflicts. They agree to certain behavioural rules set by the facilitator in advance relating to mutual respect and other such factors. It is assumed that the parties to the dispute desire a change in the status quo in favour of peaceful resolution of conflict. If one of them has already decided to dictate terms through war or otherwise and is certain not to entertain any negotiated approach, there is no scope for such a workshop.

Although Conflict Resolution Workshops are about communication between parties to a dispute, the objective is not to promote communication or dialogue as an end in itself. The facilitator does not propose solution. He facilitates the interaction between the opposite parties in such a way that solutions or some convergence automatically emerges. Conflict Resolution Workshops are closely linked to the larger political process. Selection of participants and definition of the agenda are based on careful analysis of the current political situation within and between the conflicting parties. The objective of the Workshop is to generate input into the political process, including the decision-making process and political debate within each country. Sometimes Conflict Resolution Workshops prepare the ground for official dialogue between conflicting parties.

It is necessary to bear in mind the difference between official negotiations and Conflict Resolution Workshops. The former alone can produce binding agreements but they are so rigid that it is difficult to explore ideas which could perhaps lead to binding agreements. Conflict Resolution Workshops provide such flexibility but the understanding reached there cannot be in the form of binding agreements. It must be communicated to official decision-makers so that the latter can negotiate agreements. Thus, workshops serve two purposes. One, they have an impact on the participants themselves and their perceptions of the 'enemy image' of the other side, their understanding of the dynamics of conflicts, and their insight into new ideas for resolution. Two, they generate the possibility of pro-peace ideas being fed into the political process.

The workshop may be convened or sponsored by any peace research or action centre capable of inviting responsible political leaders to its forum. There should be a panel of facilitators. The parties to the dispute may be represented by 3 to 10 persons each if there are two parties and 3 to 5 persons if there are more than two parties. The workshop lasts two to three days as this is all the time responsible political leaders can be expected to spend. Besides the business conducted on the table, there should be enough scope for informal interaction over lunches, dinners and coffee breaks. Certain guidelines must be observed by all actors in the process.

Actors	*Tools*
—Sponsors	—Lectures
—Facilitators	—Discussions

—Parties to the dispute   —Simulations
                             —Role reversals
                             —Working groups
                             —Reading material
                             —Case-studies

Guidelines for Sponsors

—Ensure adequate funds and logistical support
—Identify a neutral location which is also convenient for the participants
—Consult parties to the dispute regarding seating arrangements
—Ensure that observers and media persons are not present except, perhaps, at inaugural and concluding plenaries
—Arrange for interpreters if necessary
—Provide for small conference rooms near the main meeting place in which the parties can meet separately
—Circulate lists of parties and facilitators
—Ensure adequate consultations with parties to the dispute in advance about rules of the game
—Ensure qualified and respectable facilitators
—Be flexible in changing the agenda as desired by facilitators and parties to the dispute
—Take responsibility for follow-up action and communication

Guidelines for Facilitators

—Clarify if the facilitator is only a facilitator or also a mediator
—If the facilitator is only a facilitator, no mediation should be imposed
—Do not try to seek compromises. But facilitate analysis so that goals and tactics, interests, values and needs, can be clarified, which could later help deduce possible outcomes on the basis of the analysis made
—Facilitators should have adequate knowledge of conflict theories and experience in facilitation process
—There should be a panel of facilitators since one facilitator

can get tired
—Do not include a person who has taken a public stand on the issue, advocating the views of one of the parties to the dispute or otherwise may have motivation to be biased
—The members of the panel of facilitators should consult each other before and in breaks during the workshop for clarification and coherence
—Meet each party in advance and explain the objectives as well as procedures
—Do not respond to any secret lobbying if resorted to by any party to the dispute
—Do not have own agenda
—Show appropriate respect to all representatives of parties to the dispute; be sensitive to audience response
—Do not take sides

Guidelines for Representatives of Parties to the Dispute

—The representatives should be selected for their calibre and access to leadership but they should not be leaders themselves
—The representative team should include different factions within a party to the dispute (e.g. different communities or different political parties within a country)
—Maintain confidentiality of the substance of discussion outside the conference room
—Observe rules of procedure as agreed upon in advance
—Resist from presenting any proposal for solution until the analysis of the situation is complete and a definition of the situation is agreed upon.
—Listen to the initial presentation by the other party without interruption—ask for clarification after the presentation is complete
—Adapt analytical approach; do not indulge in point-scoring debates
—Have full discussion among members of the party before and during workshop
—Speak to each other; not to constituencies back home

Guidelines for a Series of Workshops

In the first workshop, direct discussion should focus on
- definition of the conflict
- options for each party for resolution including immediate steps

In the following workshops discussion should be on
- options and steps from immediate to intermediate to long term
- Allow enough time in between workshops to facilitate consultations between representatives and their leaders or constituencies
- Have substantially the same teams of representatives
- Each meeting should build on the last so that there is a natural progression from analysis of the conflict to deduction of options and steps to be undertaken

Agenda for Workshops

In Chapter 1, it was mentioned that a Workshop may be 'introductory' or 'substantive'. Model agendas would vary depending on the type of the Workshop.

Workshop I: Introductory

Evening before	-	Reception; introduction by participants
Day 1 / a.m.	-	Opening statements by a dignitary, sponsors and facilitators explaining the objectives and agenda
	-	Simulation exercise to break the ice
Day 1 / p.m.	-	Presentation on major issues facing parties to the dispute; discussion
	-	Case studies of conflict resolution
Day 2 / a.m.	-	Analysis of conflicts, barriers to negotiations, difference between conflict settlement and resolution
	-	Issue-based working groups
Day 2 / p.m.	-	Issue-based working groups (*contd*)
	-	Presentations by working groups
	-	Advanced simulation exercise
Day 3 / a.m.	-	Discussion on the role of parliamentar-

	ians and other political leaders—limits and strengths
	- Case-studies of conflict resolution
Day 3 / p.m.	- Follow-up actions and continued communications

Workshop II: Substantive

Evening before	- Reception; introduction by all participants; their expectations from the workshop
Day 1 / a.m.	- Opening statement by each side
	- Clarification related to opening statements
	- Discussion on central concerns and goals of each side
Day 1 / p.m.	- Statement by facilitators on shared and unshared elements in respective approaches; presentation of the statement to the plenary; discussion
	- Definition of the conflict by each party to the dispute
	- Case-studies from outside the region or from history of the region
Day 2 / a.m.	- Presentation by each side on possible solution; their own willingness for change in structures, institutions and policies
	- Identification of commonality by facilitators and their perceptions on required changes in structures, institutions and policies by each side - immediate steps, transitional steps as well as longer term solutions
	- Discussion on constraints on solutions (and their consequences)
Day 2 / p.m.	- Focussed discussion on immediate steps and means of continued communication until the next meeting; follow-up actions

4

Report on the Maldives Workshop

PARLIAMENTARIANS for Global Action and the International Centre for Peace Initiatives with the International Peace Academy organized a workshop for South Asian parliamentarians in the Maldives in May 1995. The following lessons were learnt from it which may be useful for others who may want to organize a similar workshop.

1. Be clear about the objective of the workshop.

It is mentioned in the earlier chapter that the workshop may be (1) introductory or (2) substantive. Since this was the first major conflict resolution workshop to be held in South Asia for parliamentarians, it was decided that the objective would be introductory. In other words, the emphasis was on introducing conflict resolution concepts and techniques. It was not meant directly to contribute to the resolution of any specific conflict in the region. It was decided to make a provision of working groups when specific conflicts might be addressed by the participants.

It is necessary to state the specific objectives of the workshop openly on the first day and constantly assess the proceedings with reference to the objectives.

2. Involve local actors in conceptualization and planning.

Since the beginning, Global Action involved the Bombay-based International Centre for Peace Initiatives as the regional coordinating agency for the project. It was also decided to form a steering committee of eminent persons from the region to guide the project. The following factors were borne in mind while approaching various persons for steering committee membership:

—That they should be respected within their own country and also in other countries in the region

—That they would be reputed for their ability to overcome partisan loyalties for a greater cause

—That they would agree to contribute to the conflict resolution process and not use the platform offered by the project to promote national or partisan interests which could accentuate conflicts.

3. Be balanced.

The steering committee had members from all South Asian countries. It was also balanced between parliamentarians and conflict resolution experts. It would have been ideal to have more women to achieve gender balance though this objective was not achieved.

4. Be careful in the choice of location for workshops.

It is important to find a neutral location. Since in South Asia India, Pakistan and Bangladesh are involved in various conflicts, Nepal and the Maldives were chosen for the planning and main workshops respectively. It is necessary to involve a local body to facilitate logistics, protocol and other needs. The Citizens' Majlis of the Maldives was invited to be the co-host of the main workshop which ensured smooth functioning. The need to involve local authorities of the host country makes it all the more necessary that the host country is neutral.

5. Combine process knowhow and political realities.

The programme of the main workshop was prepared taking into account the requirements of conflict resolution discipline and political realities in the region. The steering committee played a key role in drafting the agenda.

It was found that the participants were not much interested in simulation exercises. If the participants are political leaders, it is better to devote much time for discussion of concepts and issues, case studies and working groups to address real problems. If the participants are academics, they may appreciate a higher dose of simulation exercises.

6. Be balanced in the selection of participants.

It was decided to invite equal number (four) of participants from each country (1) from all major sections of the political spectrum (2) including at least one woman in each delegation and (3) relatively young.

In order to have multiplier impact, it was decided that the participants would be influential in their party structures. In order to avoid over-politicization of discussions, it was decided that the participants would *NOT* be frontline leaders. In other words, the focus was on identifying second rank or middle level leaders with good standing with the top party leadership.

It was also decided to invite only those parliamentarians who would be interested in the conflict resolution process.

7. Engage reputed resource persons.

It is important to have resource persons who would be able to command respect of the participants, who would not be biased and who would be in a position to control tensions.

8. Have a limited time-frame.

It is difficult for politicians to spare much time. The Maldives workshop was planned for five days, but many key participants found it impossible to stay for the last day. The ideal duration should be 3 days with an additional day before the workshop for arrival and welcome reception. If participants are advisors to political parties or academics, they may be willing to attend a workshop for 4 to 5 days.

9. Provide time for informal interactions.

A workshop only provides a structured setting. It is necessary for participants to get to know each other at a personal level which can contribute a lot to break prejudices and develop human bonds. The programme should not be overcrowded so that the participants have some opportunity for informal interaction. Such informal sessions can also be used to resolve problems which might come up in the official agenda.

10. Be flexible.

The Maldives workshop programme was changed several times to suit the needs of the participants. Since the participants understood basic concepts very quickly, they wanted to spend more time in addressing real issues and planning concrete follow-up actions.

11. Concentrate on follow-up actions.

A workshop should be result-oriented. Unlike a seminar where issues are discussed and a few recommendations are made on substantive issues, a workshop should be aimed at concrete actions. If the workshop is introductory, it may be decided to hold a follow-up workshop which could be substantive. There may be decisions about follow-up communications between participants. In the Maldives workshop, the participants showed an interest in participating in another, more intensive, workshop. The Indian and Pakistani participants reached agreement on a process to break communication barriers between leaders of the two countries.

The full report of the workshop is given below to give an idea of what transpired and how.

Executive Summary

Parliamentarians for Global Action and the International Centre for Peace Initiatives in cooperation with the International Peace Academy had organized a workshop for parliamentarians from South Asia with a view to building political capacity for peace-making in the region. The workshop was held at the Bandos Island Resort in the Maldives from May 19 to 23, 1995. It was co-hosted by the Citizens Majlis of the Maldives and inaugurated by Mr Maumoon Abdul Gayoom, President of the Maldives. It was attended by 30 political leaders and experts including 10 serving or former ministers from Bangladesh, India, Nepal, Maldives, Pakistan and Sri Lanka.

1. The workshop brought together political leaders from six South Asian countries specifically to discuss the resolution of bilateral, subregional and regional conflicts.

2. The workshop participants were made familiar with conflict resolution concepts, techniques and skills through a series of exercises, simulations and discussions.

3. The workshop resulted in the following concrete decisions:

—A follow-up process of exchange of views between parliamentarians from India and Bangladesh on the conflict
over water resources (this decision was eventually
dropped in the course of follow-up action since soon
after the Maldives workshop, Indo-Bangladesh dialogues
on water resources were initiated at official as well as
track two levels).

—A continuous, uninterrupted, unconditional dialogue
between nominees of the leaders of Indian and Pakistani
political parties with no commitment from either side
except the commitment to engage in the dialogue on a
regular basis with a view to address critical issues in
bilateral relations.

—National parliamentary groups and national workshops
on peace and cooperation; national groups to be linked
in a regional forum.

—A network of women political and civic leaders from
the region to promote peaceful resolution of conflicts
and cooperation.

—Publication of a handbook on the role of parliamentarians in conflict resolution, distribution of issue briefs by
Global Action, and the exchange of views between parliamentarians from different countries through the journal of Peace Initiatives.

—The development of the concept of South Asian Parliament.

4. In the inauguration of the workshop, Mr Maumoon Abdul
Gayoom, President of the Maldives, highlighted a new
approach towards regional security

—which precludes the use of weapons and means which
could result in the suffering of innocent civilians;

—which encourages humanitarian actions in conflict-ridden areas irrespective of any political positions or ideologies;

—which prohibits terrorism, illicit transfer of arms and
narcotic drugs, and the harbouring and training of politically motivated elements;

—which gives consideration to the concerns of small states in the region.

He asked the political leaders to pursue these objectives in their parliaments.

5. The participants developed intimate personal relations and understanding which were very evident throughout the course of the workshop.

Background

Since the establishment of South Asian Association for Regional Cooperation (SAARC) in 1980, the non-governmental community in South Asia has been active in efforts to promote regional cooperation. Since 1990 it has also been engaged in efforts to search for peaceful solutions to conflicts in the region. But most of the non-governmental players include scholars, retired government officers and personnel from armed forces and journalists. The ability of these players to influence decision-making processes is limited.

It was therefore decided by the International Centre for Peace Initiatives (ICPI) in 1993 to engage parliamentarians and political leaders in the peace-making process. The ICPI approached Parliamentarians for Global Action (PGA) which has an international network of parliamentarians committed to peace and world reform. The two organizations decided to invite the International Peace Academy (IPA) which has technical expertise in conflict resolution techniques.

The special strengths the parliamentarians have include the rights and opportunities to

- propose legislation and resolutions in parliament aimed at resolving conflict and reducing tensions;
- deliver speeches in parliament which advocate peaceful solutions and reduce tensions;
- conduct electoral political campaigns using language in a manner which reduces antagonism;
- use political leverage and access to party leadership in mobilizing government support for peaceful solutions;
- take public initiatives to promote peace in the general public as well as in their regional constituencies.

While exploring the scope for political leaders to perform peace-making functions, it would be necessary to bear in mind that they would need preparation for successful implementation of such tasks through the strengthening of their knowledge, skills and techniques. Second, they might not have adequate time to make such preparations as they have multiple obligations towards their parliament, constituency, party, etc.

Keeping in mind the above-mentioned strengths and limitations of parliamentarians, the ICPI, PGA and the IPA decided to organize a series of workshops to build the capacity of parliamentarians and other political leaders.

Planning Workshop

As the first step, a planning workshop was organized at Kathmandu on May 21-22, 1994. It was attended by ten parliamentarians and conflict resolution experts from the region, besides the representatives of the three organizations. The participants formed a Steering Committee comprising themselves and decided to hold a four-day workshop for parliamentarians from Bangladesh, India, Nepal, the Maldives, Pakistan and Sri Lanka in the spring of 1995. They decided on the Maldives as the location for the workshop. They also settled the selection criteria for parliamentarians, programme content of the Maldives workshop, and roles for members of the Steering Committee. Dr Abdul Moyeen Khan, planning minister of Bangladesh, served as the chairman of the planning workshop.

Maldives Workshop Participants

As per the decision taken at Kathmandu, a workshop was held at the Maldives from May 19 to 23, 1995. The participants included

Members of Parliament	21
Former MPs and ministers	3
Regional experts (including ministers)	4
Experts from outside the region	2
Organizers and observers	4
TOTAL	34

Among the 21 MPs, there were
6 serving ministers and
4 former ministers
The list of participants is attached as Annex 1.

Inauguration Ceremony

The workshop was inaugurated by Mr Maumoon Abdul Gayoom, President of the Maldives. He called upon parliamentarians in South Asia to develop a new approach towards regional security.

President Gayoom said "Any new approach towards regional security in South Asia must take into account people's aspirations for a better tomorrow. It must preclude any use of arms and means which could result in the suffering of innocent civilians. On the other hand, it must welcome humanitarian actions in conflict-ridden areas irrespective of any political positions or ideologies. Terrorism, illicit transfer of arms and narcotic drugs, and the harbouring and training of politically motivated elements must be stopped."

He also called for increased economic co-operation among South Asian nations in order to banish poverty. He added "if we have to overcome the problem of poverty, it is imperative to divert our national energy and resources from the politics of conflict to the economics of prosperity".

Speaking earlier on the occasion, Mr Sundeep Waslekar, Director, the International Centre for Peace Initiatives, said: "The principle of the *Human Life Above All* in conflict zones must be endorsed by political leaders in South Asia. It will encourage social organizations to undertake humanitarian work to address crisis of human life in areas ravaged by conflicts."

Mr Sundeep Waslekar also proposed a new approach to regional security which prohibits the use of weapons of all kinds, especially weapons of terrorism. He added: "The SAARC Convention on Terrorism is merely an extradition treaty. It is further weakened because of contradictions between its articles VI and VII. If a meaningful protocol against terrorism is signed, it will enable the acceptance of a treaty prohibiting the use of weapons of all kinds."

Mr Abdulla Hameed, Speaker of the Citizens Majlis of the Maldives, chaired the inaugural session. Mr Murli Deora, International President of PGA, introduced President Gayoom. Dr Jean Krasno, project coordinator, proposed the vote of thanks.

Programme

The workshop programme had

—simulation exercises on bilateral and multilateral negotiations by Dr William Weisberg of Harvard University

—presentation of the following case-studies
- preventive actions by the UN in Africa (Mr F.T. Liu)
- water resources conflict between India and Nepal (Mr Pashupati Rana)
- the ethnic conflict in Sri Lanka (Mr Mangala Moonesinghe)
- Arab-Israeli conflict (Mr F.T. Liu)
- cooperative security in South Asia (Mr Abdul Sattar)
- regional cooperation in South Asia (Mr K.K. Bhargava and Mr Javed Jabbar)

—discussions on
- dynamics of conflict and co-operation
- role of parliamentarians in peace-making
- escalation of conflict and barriers to resolution

—working groups on
- water resources conflict
- India-Pakistan relations
- regional co-operation
- women's issues.

Simulations

Oil Pricing. The oil pricing simulation is an exercise which operates like a prisoner's dilemma game in which teams of participants compete with each other to sell oil and maximize profits. The process of active involvement in the simulation offered the participants direct experience in the interactive nature of competition. What each side did in one round of competition evoked a response from the other side. Non-verbal actions took on a symbolic nature which the opponent could easily misread when there was no other form of communication. The participants observed that once confidence was destroyed, it was hard to restore. The temptation to renege on an agreement and undercut the competition was strong. One team said: "When the other side defected, we saw it as a deep betrayal which left us free to retaliate in any way possible." In analyzing the exercise, one of the MPs observed that if both sides had cooperated through all the rounds of price-setting, they would have achieved the maximum joint profits possible in the game. The extra benefit in this exercise was that it proved to be a good "ice-breaker". As the first session of the workshop, it loosened up the participants, created a bond between team members, and provided for open conversation during the breaks.

The Opera. This simulation, entitled "Sally Soprano", called for a bargaining session between the agent of an aging opera singer and an opera company looking for a lead soprano. The exercise involved the participants in an active bargaining process to demonstrate the use of various negotiating skills. The participants were asked to formulate their "best alternative to a negotiated agreement" or BATNA as a back-up if the negotiations failed. They were also asked to identify the opposition's BATNA to see if there was an incentive to bargain or not. After the participants had completed the negotiations, they were asked as a group to analyze the strategy they had undertaken in the bargaining process and discuss whether they had used a distributive (zero-sum) approach or an integrative strategy. Integrative bargaining involves looking at underlying interests and seeking creative solutions which offer mutual benefits to satisfy a variety of needs on both sides.

The Water Simulation. The third simulation involved water issues and was a hypothetical scenario written for South Asia. The exercise was more complex than the previous two and involved three countries negotiating over the building of a dam on the territory of one nation which would affect the flow of water in the rivers of the other two countries. A crisis over the issue had developed and the regional security organization had called for an immediate round of talks in order to reduce tensions and find a solution to the conflict. Each participant was assigned a role in the negotiations, either in one of the countries as prime minister, foreign minister, member of parliament, etc., or as international actor, i.e., World Bank representative, head of the regional security organization, or UNDP representative. The countries first met to devise a negotiating strategy and then negotiations began.

Following the simulation, the group was asked to describe and analyze each strategy. They were asked to define their own country's interests and what they thought were the interests of the other two countries. They were asked to examine both the interests and needs of the other countries and how they might be addressed to arrive at an integrative solution. The group discussed creative incentives that might bring a country to the bargaining table which might otherwise simply be content with the status quo. The interaction during the simulation was then analyzed to see if the way each participant conducted his/her role—chairing the talks, representing his/her country at the table, presenting positions, etc.—helped or hindered the negotiating process.

Mr Weisberg points out that in multilateral negotiations, it is important to:

(1) identify key stake holders,
(2) reach internal consensus, and
(3) build multi-party coalitions.

In seeking peaceful solutions to protracted conflicts, it is the task of leaders in each country to take on the responsibility of building a consensus at home and selling the results to the people.

The simulations served as an opportunity to examine negotiation concepts and skills in an active participatory manner. Everyone became interactively involved. On the other hand, some of the key political leaders found simulations too academic. They would rather spend time on case-studies and hard issues. The lesson to be distilled is that in a workshop where top political leaders are involved, there should be one or two simulations to create participatory dynamics but simulation exercises should not be too time-consuming or overemphasized in the overall programme.

Discussion on Concepts

Following the simulations, Mr Weisberg outlined some of the impediments to principled negotiation. Strategic barriers, cognitive barriers and other psychological barriers were highlighted. An example of a strategic barrier would be a negotiator who is reluctant to share his or her underlying interests or preferences with an adversary for fear that divulging this knowledge could be used by the other side to gain advantage. This impedes principled negotiation and precludes the opportunity for joint problem-solving. One type of psychological barrier presented at the workshop was the phenomenon of partisan perceptions. Adversaries often cannot find consensus on the nature of the problem to be solved because they see reality through subjective perspectives coloured by their position in the conflict.

Mr Weisberg described how some of these obstacles to negotiation can be overcome with the use of a third party. Partisans will sometimes trust a third party with information regarding preference without the fear that this information will be used against them. The third party can then help to fashion an agreement beneficial to both without jeopardizing the interests of either party. A third party can also help adversaries overcome psychological barriers, such as the problem of partisan perceptions, by employing third party interventions that induce the parties to recognize the complex nature of reality and the existence of multiple perspectives.

The discussion on obstacles to negotiation and the methods for overcoming them led to a discussion of more advanced concepts in conflict resolution. The participants talked about these ideas in the context of their own experiences in the region. There was particular interest in discussing negotiation strategies for addressing power imbalances in conflict relationships.

In evaluating the role of parliamentarians, the group discussed the point that MPs have privileges. They can speak in parliament and have links to government. They bring messages from the people to the government and take the government's response to the people. They can also use the media. There are constraints, however. There is often no free flow of information from the government to parliament nor to the media. Government decisions are taken without consulting parliament, the Opposition or even the ruling party. MPs also often misuse the media and use it to posture and often stir up tensions and conflicts to win votes. Work needs to be done to use the role of MPs in a more positive way and this project can help that process.

Case Histories and Issue Presentations

Integrated into the workshop agenda along with the development of skills were a number of case histories involving conflict and the presentation of issues specific to the region. Mr F.T. Liu, former UN Assistant Secretary-General for Special Political Affairs, gave an overview of conflict prevention and the role of the UN. He also gave a case history of the Arab-Israeli conflict along with an account of periodic efforts to resolve the conflict. One of the participants related a history of ethnic difficulties in Sri Lanka and efforts to mediate the conflict. Another participant presented his thoughts on water issues in the region and efforts to address disputes which continue to remain unresolved.

Several of the participants presented their views and experiences in developing cooperation in the region. Both Mr Ibrahim Zaki and Mr K.K. Bhargava, members of the Steering Committee, have been former Secretaries-General of SAARC. They each spoke of their experiences in trying to achieve levels of cooperation in the region. The ten years of the organization's existence have shown some incremental achievements in cooperation, but both agreed that there have been major constraints on the organization which have impeded its success. Mr Abdul Sattar, former Foreign Minister of Pakistan, spoke about various efforts to reach levels of cooperation between Pakistan and India and the difficulties faced by the two countries in reaching an understanding.

Working Groups

The working groups had the mandate to outline follow-up

actions.

1. The working group on regional cooperation reached the following conclusions:

   —Individual interested members in each national parliament might form a group devoted to the promotion of regional co-operation.

   —Parliamentary groups from South Asian countries might form a regional forum.

   —The forum might meet once or more often each year and make recommendations to the SAARC Council of Ministers and leaders on issues of regional concern.

   —The forum might set up specialized consultative committees to address specific issues such as trade, environment, human rights, social reforms.

   —Each parliament should hold periodical discussions on regional cooperation. Committees of the parliaments dealing with foreign affairs may do the same.

   —The SAARC Secretariat might prepare and disseminate an information bulletin for the benefit of parliaments.

   —The SAARC focal points in the foreign offices of each country may periodically brief the parliamentary forum on regional cooperation.

2. The working group on India-Pakistan relations decided to institute a continuous, uninterrupted, unconditional dialogue between leaders of political parties in India and Pakistan with no commitment on either side except the commitment to engage in the dialogue on a regular basis. The dialogue will have the following features:

   • from each side, 4 or 5 parties will be invited to participate

   • the leaders of the parties will nominate two official representatives

   • the representatives may or may not be members of parliament but they will essentially represent their leaders and speak for them

   • Mr Sundeep Waslekar will hold consultations with the leaders of Indian parties and Mr Javed Jabbar will hold consultations with the leaders of Pakistani parties

- Mr Waslekar and Mr Jabbar will discuss logistics as soon as they have sought the consent of political leaders to the dialogue and the nominees of the leaders have been identified
- assuming that several months are required for preparatory work, the first round of dialogue will take place in 1996

3. The working group on water resources conflict decided that the Indian and Bangladeshi parliamentarians, on their return to capitals,
   - will study national perspectives on the subject
   - will exchange visits of three parliamentarians from each side
   - will try to identify peaceful solutions which will serve mutual interest.

4. The working group on women's issues decided to promote measures which will uphold women's dignity, encourage discussion in the parliaments on women's issues and promote the role of women in conflict resolution.

Plenary on Political Action

The plenary on political action

- endorsed all of the above decisions of the working groups
- endorsed the decision to produce a Handbook on the Role of Parliamentarians in Conflict Resolution
- requested members to send comments on the proposal for the South Asian Parliament to the ICPI office
- requested members to contribute to the journal of Peace Initiatives to facilitate exchange of views
- advised the proposed regional forum of parliamentary groups on peace and cooperation to keep in contact with the SAARC Secretariat, SAARC Chamber and other regional institutions.

Evaluation

In general, the goals of the workshop were achieved: the selected group of parliamentarians and leaders brought together from the region, through exercises and case histories designed for the workshop, enhanced their capacity to seek peaceful solutions to conflicts in the region and formed working groups to focus on follow-up activities on issues in South Asia. The selection process established by the Steering Committee was sound as borne out by the high level of participation and the degree of commitment to seeking peaceful cooperation demonstrated by the open dialogue and eagerness to move forward in the working groups.

The participants were asked to evaluate the workshop themselves and they did so both verbally and in writing. In discussing the workshop during the last session, they all said that the experience had been rewarding and useful. They wanted to continue the project and meet again in a few months for a second workshop. One recurring comment was that the workshop had provided an opportunity to hear about issues from another perspective. One participant said: "We in parliament often don't have time to do the research we need in order to make our decisions. What we have learned here is very useful. Some very positive steps have been taken. The emotional feelings and attachments we have made will reduce tensions and build confidence in the region."

One of the women said, "This workshop was run in a very democratic way. We talked about women's issues and the men were supportive; this is a milestone." She later explained that in her parliament women are rarely allowed to speak and are often kept uninformed on proposed legislation. Another MP stated that the things he had learned would help him in any track two diplomacy he would undertake. One participant who is committed to be involved in the follow-up work said: "We plan to spread this knowledge beyond this effort." An MP explained that while the goals of the workshop had been achieved, he felt he didn't "have time to absorb all the skills internally." Therefore, he recommended the same group meet again in a few months to continue the process. The other participants readily agreed.

Another member of the group suggested that there be fewer simulations. The group generally liked the oil pricing exercise but did not like the one on the opera. They felt it was too removed from the region and was too simplistic. The water simulation was more relevant to the issues of the region. It was suggested that in the next workshop the simulations, when used, should be based on issues in the region. One member said that the next workshop "should go into depth on how water issues have been settled in other regions. Resource people who are experts in the field should be invited." Another participant said: "Mr William Weisberg expanded our minds here. His sincerity helped to build our capacities and our resolve." One of the MPs summed up the sentiment when he said that "a village" had been created here which included all religions, cultures, and faiths of the region.

In written evaluations everyone said the workshop was useful and many said they would be able to apply the concepts to the work they were doing in their country and in the region. Others hoped they would be able to use the concepts. They found the case studies and simulations useful but some wanted the simulations to reflect more of the issues of the region. Others suggested that the next workshop ought to focus more directly on ethnic conflict and how to negotiate in ways that could overcome difficult and intractable issues.

Conclusion

The fact that leading parliamentarians representing all major political parties in South Asia met was itself an achievement. The South Asia political leaders meet at international conferences. But it was a rare occasion for them to meet exclusively in a regional forum to discuss peaceful solutions to bilateral, sub-regional and regional conflicts.

President Maumoon Abdul Gayoom, who inaugurated the workshop, set the tone by proposing a new approach towards regional security which precludes the use of weapons of all kinds, encourages humanitarian actions in conflict zones, and prohibits terrorism and transfer of illicit arms. The president's address provided valuable political objectives for the parliamentarians to pursue.

The workshop provided the knowledge of conflict analysis and negotiation techniques which the participants can use in the future.

The workshop has set in motion processes to address bilateral conflicts which create tensions and cause the arms race in the region. If the mechanisms work in an effective manner, the demand for arms should go down.

The workshop is expected to lead to the establishment of parliamentary groups on peace and cooperation which will provide support for peaceful solutions to conflicts.

The workshop provided valuable input for various publications which will be prepared in due course and made available to political leaders for strengthening their knowledge base and to all institutions interested in organizing such workshops.

As a result of the new approach, knowledge of techniques, practical mechanisms, support groups and publications, the workshop has set a new agenda for peace-making in South Asia. It has introduced innovation in the conduct of diplomacy by creating a linkage between track one and track two diplomacy. The ultimate success depends upon the follow-up that the ICPI may undertake with the support of other institutions in this task. Peace is an ongoing process. And the tasks set by the Maldives workshop demonstrate that there is no final deadline for peace, especially in South Asia.

Annex I
List of Participants

Participating Members of Parliament
(* indicates MP who is a member of the Steering Committee)

Bangladesh
Ms Mamia Ching, MP
Mr Ataur Rahman Khan, MP

India
*Mr Pramod Mahajan, MP
Mr Som Pal, MP
Mr Murli Deora, MP

Maldives
Mr N.D. Abdul Hameed Abdul Hakeem, MP
Mr K.D. Ahmed Manik, MP
Mrs Fathimath Sheerin, MP
Mr Ahmed Zahir, MP

Nepal
Mr Jhala Nath Khanal, MP
Mr Arjun Narsingha K.C., MP
Ms Sahana Pradhan, MP
*Mr Pashupati Shumshere Rana, MP

Pakistan
Mr Aitzaz Ahsan, MP
Ms Tehmina Daultana, MP
Mr Syed Naveed Qamar, MP
Mr Mehmood Khan Achakzai, MP

Sri Lanka
Mrs R.M. Pulendran, MP
Mr W.D.J. Seneviratne, MP

Mr Arunasalam Thangathuraj, MP
Mr Wisva Warnapala, MP

Steering Committee Members
Mr K.K. Bhargava
India
Friedrich Ebert Foundation

Mr Javed Jabbar
Pakistan
Chairman, South Asian Media Association
Former Minister of Information and Broadcasting

Mr Mangala Moonesinghe
Sri Lanka
High Commissioner to India

Mr Ahmed Saleem
Maldives
Director-General, Ministry of Youth, Women's Affairs and
Sports

Prof K.B. Singh
Nepal
Centre for Strategic and International Studies

Mr Sundeep Waslekar
India
International Centre for Peace Initiatives

Mr Ibrahim Hussan Zaki
Maldives
Minister of Tourism

Experts
Mr F.T. Liu
Special Advisor, International Peace Academy

Former UN Assistant Secretary-General for Special Political
Affairs

Mr Abdul Sattar
Former Foreign Minister, Pakistan

Mr William Weisberg
Harvard University
Program on International Conflict Analysis and Resolution

PGA Staff Members
Dr Jean Krasno
Program Officer
Peacekeeping and Collective Security

Mr Andrew Fried
Program Assistant

Observer
Mr Subramaniam Ayer
Shree Bhikshu Foundation

5

Inaugural Statements

AT a political workshop it is a good idea to have two or three statements at the inauguration ceremony. One statement should be made on behalf of the organizers. One or two statements should be made by a distinguished personality in the region whose words may be respected by all the participants.

The purpose of the inaugural statements is to explain the objectives of the workshop, set a constructive tone and provide political direction.

The organizer's statement should focus on the objectives and expectations from the workshop. The distinguished personality's statement should be of a normative nature in terms of political substance. If possible, there should be preparatory consultations between the two persons making the respective statements to develop a common approach.

At the Maldives workshop, Mr Sundeep Waslekar, the ICPI Director, made the statement on behalf of organizers. His Excellency Mr Maumoon Abdul Gayoom, President of the Maldives, was invited to present his views as a senior statesman.

Mr Waslekar explained the context of the workshop and spelt out possible outcomes which the participants could strive for. President Gayoom recommended political actions to be pursued by the participants. Both called for a new framework for regional security in South Asia. Mr Waslekar made certain proposals. President Gayoom responded to some of them immediately. This was possible due to prior consultations between the International Centre for Peace Initiatives and the President's secretariat.

Text of Mr Sundeep Waslekar's speech at the inauguration of the workshop on Political Capacity-building for Peace-making in South Asia at Islamic Centre, Male, the Maldives, on May 20, 1995

Twenty five years ago, when I was about ten years old, I used to live in a township near Bombay. One day communal riots broke out in our town. Hindus and Muslims were literally burning each other. My family was living in a Hindu neighbourhood. But we had a Muslim family living next door. In the afternoon, a Hindu militant mob approached us to set the next door Muslim family on fire. At that stage, my grandmother provided shelter to the neighbours and dared the mob to set her on fire first. The Hindu mob did not touch the old woman. One by one the militants bowed their heads and disappeared. On that day I, as a child, learnt that *peace is possible*.

What I learnt as a child was not too different from what I now learn as a student of human relations. Camp David accord, the INF treaty, Arias plan in Central America, the Middle East process, recent developments in northern Ireland and South Africa all prove that peace is possible. This is not to suggest that there have been no problems with some of the peace accords. The challenge in maintaining peace achieved with much effort proves that peace has no fixed definition of achievement. Peace has no finishing line, no final deadline.

Here the representatives of South Asian people are meeting to discuss how peace can be made possible in the region. This is a democratic moment in South Asia. In modern history, no two democracies have ever been engaged in war. But absence of war is not peace. If a democracy really has to work for the benefit and welfare of people, it is important that even fear of war and causes of such fear are eliminated from the psyche of a nation. Earlier wars used to take place to annex or protect territories and resources. These days they take place in the name of human aspirations. But the results of conflicts in Afganisthan, Central America, Bosnia, Somalia, Rwanda, all prove how violent conflict is a powerless and ineffective instrument of realizing human aspirations.

Those who have the ability to see the futility of conflict must also be able to overcome their obsession with the past. People of South Asia, and people everywhere else, are aspiring for a better future. All those investors whom South Asian governments are trying to attract do not want to know what happened in 1949 or 1971 or 1987. They want to know what is going to happen in 1997 so that they can decide whether to put their billions on South Asia's tables.

The initiative to build political capacity in South Asia is an invitation to begin the history. It is a call for a journey to a new future. In the last few years, many track two diplomatic activities have mushroomed in the region. They demonstrate the ability of South Asia's concerned citizens to break old mental frameworks and begin to build new ones. The support of local philanthropists such as Shree Bhikshu Foundation demonstrates emerging interest of South Asia's economic actors in a peaceful polity. Of course, critics may argue that such support is limited. But a beginning is to be made. And in a half filled glass, I would rather notice the water than the empty space.

Track two diplomacy must be distinguished from well-meaning exercises aimed at improving people-to-people contacts. While the latter do not necessarily have a direct impact on the policy making processes, track two diplomacy may be defined as a process of dialogue between those who are outside the government machinery but whose voices are heard and respected by policy-makers. Retired civil servants and reputed scholars have attempted track two diplomacy. But they have limitations. On the other hand, parliamentarians have several constitutional and political strengths. For instance, you understand public preferences more directly than civil servants do. You can also mobilize public opinion in support of a cause. You have legislative privileges to move resolutions and pass bills binding the governments and people of the country. You have qualitative access to party leaders and heads of governments. And who knows, in a few years, some of you may become heads of governments and Opposition parties.

It is up to you to use these strengths for your people. The conceptual skills and techniques of conflict resolution you will acquire can be utilized to turn the wheel of South Asia's history.

It should be possible for you to agree on at least some principles, and then work together to persuade your governments and people to support them.

One principle I would appeal to you to examine relates to the impact of violent conflicts on human life. While powerful elements in society engineer a conflict, the victims are innocent citizens. Innocent children are orphaned. Women are widowed. Citizens are deprived of health care, education, employment. As political leaders, you should encourage social organizations to undertake humanitarian work to address crisis of human life in areas ravaged by conflicts. You should also find it possible to agree to request your governments and their agencies not to obstruct humanitarian work undertaken by voluntary bodies to alleviate the suffering of victims of violent conflicts. The principle of Human Life Above All in conflict zones, endorsed by you, may invoke positive response from voluntary organizations in the region who may come forward in a large number.

The second principle you may consider could involve a new approach to regional security which prohibits the use of weapons of all kinds. India and Pakistan, the two largest adversaries in the region, have negotiated no-war pacts or joint defence agreements in 1949-50, 1953, 1956, 1959, 1968, 1969, 1974, 1977 and the 1980s. They can build on the past efforts and negotiate a new treaty renouncing the use of weapons of all kinds. Perhaps, a regional treaty can be envisaged which also takes into account the security concerns of other states. For such a treaty to work, it is necessary to have a protocol compelling states to take steps not to allow people or territory under their jurisdiction to cause violence anywhere else in the region. The SAARC Convention on Terrorism is merely an extradition treaty. It is further weakened because of contradictions between its articles VI and VII. If a meaningful protocol against terrorism is signed, it will enable the passage of a treaty prohibiting the use of weapons of all kinds. Parliamentarians can take a lead in this matter.

Another principle you may find it easy to consider should relate to improvement in communication between people and their representatives in the region. This can be supported by concrete practical actions. The parliamentarians present here, and their colleagues back home, can form bilateral working groups to address conflicts and arms race between their countries. For instance, Indian and Pakistani parliamentarians can form a bilateral group which meets at a regular interval, in sun or in rains, to discuss critical issues dividing their countries, to explore possibilities of reducing tensions and to lower the demand for arms race. Similar groups can be formed by MPs from any two countries in dispute. As far as sub-regional or regional issues are concerned, multilateral working groups can be formed according to the scope of the issue.

In brief, you can go back from the Maldives with three types of results. One, you will have acquired better knowledge and awareness of concepts, skills and techniques of conflict resolution. Two, you can agree on certain principles for the conduct of inter-state relations within the region. Three, you can establish mechanisms to improve communication and dialogue on critical issues. If you achieve these results, you will have launched a new peace process in South Asia. This may be an opportunity to begin the history in this region. If peace prevails, it will be possible to prevent the proliferation of poverty. Peace or poverty? If you ask the one billion people of this region, their answer would be obvious. Finally, I would like to share a people's view on conflicts in our region. It was explained by an engineer in the Karachi Steel Mill. He said: "When Allah was distributing intelligence, all people in South Asia were sitting in the first row. So, we are intelligent people. But when Allah started distributing wisdom, everyone from Peshawar to Chittagong disappeared. So, we are not very wise people." Distinguished Members of Parliament, I appeal to you to be as wise as you are intelligent. And we shall overcome.

Inaugural Address by His Excellency Mr Maumoon Abdul Gayoom, President of the Republic of Maldives, at the Workshop on Political Capacity-building for Peace-making in South Asia at Male on 20 May 1995

Honourable Speaker of the Citizens' Majlis, Honourable Ministers, Distinguished Parliamentarians, Ladies and Gentlemen:

It gives me great pleasure to welcome the distinguished Members of Parliament and other participants in this workshop on political capacity-building for peace-making in South Asia. I thank the Parliamentarians for Global Action, the International Centre for Peace Initiatives and the International Peace Academy, for organizing this event in the Maldives. It reflects their confidence in our commitment to peace. This workshop is being co-hosted by the Citizens' Majlis, whose distinguished members, I am sure, will benefit from its proceedings.

Two weeks ago, I participated in the Eighth SAARC Summit. One important decision taken at the meeting was to designate 1995 as the year for eradicating poverty. We owe it to our children and their children to banish poverty from this region. If we have to overcome the problem of poverty, it is imperative to divert our national energy and resources from the politics of conflict to the economics of prosperity. Proliferation of weapons and proliferation of poverty go hand in hand.

Enhancing the United Nations' collective security system, promoting confidence-building measures and engaging in preventive diplomacy are key alternatives to the arms race. The establishment of zones of peace and nuclear weapon-free zones and the prevention of the proliferation of both conventional and nuclear arms are also actions that will contribute significantly to the process of disarmament.

The United Nations, whose purpose and principles are based on the objective of maintaining international peace and security, has been involved in peace-keeping for half a century. While it is celebrating its fiftieth anniversary this year, the United Nations will have to come to terms with the fact that peace-keeping is an extremely costly affair both in terms of human life and financial resources. The number of peace-keeping operations has never been greater or more expensive. And the need for the Organisation to be more vibrant and more effective has never been more acute. I am confident that with the present efforts to restructure and revitalize the United Nations, its peace-keeping role will be further strengthened in the years and decades to come.

Security is a very special type of commodity. It increases when it is shared. This feature of security applies in a very special way to neighbourly relations. If one neighbour acts in a manner that make the others feel secure, that particular neighbour's own security is bound to increase on account of reciprocation.

The Maldives is in the happy position of being one of the few countries in the world which have no internal conflicts or disputes with any other country. Our society is homogeneous and our relations with our neighbours and with the rest of the world are firmly based on friendship and close cooperation in all areas of mutual interest. We owe this happy situation not only to the geographical location of our country and the peaceful nature of its people, but also to the genuine goodwill of our neighbours and all other countries.

The Charter of the United Nations encourages the establishment of regional peace and security arrangements. There are a number of such mechanisms functioning in various parts of the world. South Asia is one of the few regions of the world where a regional security arrangement has not been attempted. The nature of the bilateral tensions that exist in the region could well be the reason. But due to the climate of instability caused by heavily armed militant groups, small states of the region may have to face crisis situations. What happened in the Maldives in 1988 is a case in point. It is worth noting that the United Nations General Assembly resolution initiated by the Maldives entitled "Protection and Security of Small States", enabled appeals to the relevant regional and international organizations to provide assistance when requested by small states for the strengthening of their security.

The small states security initiative that the Maldives took at the UN in 1989 was an attempt to explore ways of enhancing the security of small states within a framework of multilateral cooperation. Our immediate concern was, of course, the terrorist attack on the Maldives. At that critical time, we found that all our friends were extremely supportive and willing to come to our help. However, in the absence of a regional security arrangement, it was the timely assistance of India that was instrumental in restoring peace in the country, which the people of the Maldives will always remember with sincere gratitude. The bitter experience dramatically highlighted the need for institutionalized security for small states. Such security, based on the precepts of transparency, reciprocity and international cooperation, is in line with the "new thinking" on security that has gained currency since the late 1980s.

Given the evolving international security framework, parliamentarians have a special responsibility for introducing innovation in regional security management and for working towards the peaceful solution of disputes. I am sure that this workshop can make a significant contribution to this effort. I hope that you will not only focus on skills in peace-making, but also agree on specific objectives which you can pursue in your parliaments.

Any new approach towards regional security and conflict resolution in South Asia must take into account people's aspirations for a better tomorrow. It must preclude any use of arms and means which could result in the suffering of the innocent civilians. On the other hand, it must welcome humanitarian actions in conflict-ridden areas irrespective of any political positions or ideologies. It should particularly give consideration to the concerns of small communities and small states in the region.

The real enemies of the people of South Asia are poverty, ignorance, disease and the ecological crisis. These stumbling blocks are causing social and economic stagnation, while the rest of the world is engaged in single-minded pursuit of economic advancement. In South Asia, too, communal strife and bilateral disputes must be replaced by peace, understanding and cooperation. The restoration and protection of the rights of minorities, coordination of economic policies and the promotion of joint ventures and investments among nations must be encouraged.

Terrorism, illicit transfer of arms and narcotic drugs, and the harbouring and training of politically motivated elements must be stopped.

Mr Speaker, Honourable Ministers, Distinguished Parliamentarians, Ladies and Gentlemen:

We are living in a rapidly changing world. Social, economic, cultural and political changes are taking place at an accelerating speed. If we do not ride the wave of change, we will be left behind. To survive and succeed, we have to arm ourselves not with weapons of destruction but with knowledge. With knowledge come new ideas and new relationships and new ways of solving problems. In the international arena, resolution of conflicts by war is giving way to the resolution of conflicts by dialogue and compromise. The Cold War, the problem of Southern Africa and, to a certain degree, the question of Palestine are clear examples.

As knowledge has become the new source of power, we must realize that in the coming year and decades, the mentality of the survival of the fittest or the most powerful will inevitably be replaced by the belief in the survival of the wisest. Peace now and in the future can be achieved only by reason, knowledge, cooperation and compromise. Compromise means sacrifice. When the reward is national harmony or peace among nations, no sacrifice is too great a price to pay.

The United Nations Secretary-General Dr Boutros Boutros-Ghali, said in his report entitled "An Agenda for Peace": "Globalism and nationalism need not be viewed as opposing trends, doomed to spur each other on to extremes of reaction. The healthy globalization of contemporary life requires in the first instance solid identities and fundamental freedoms. The sovereignty, territorial integrity and independence of States within the established international system, and the principle of self-determination of people, both of great value and importance, must not be permitted to work against each other in the period ahead. Respect for democratic principles at all levels of social existence is crucial: in communities, within States and within the community of States. Our constant duty should be to maintain the integrity of each while finding a balanced design for all."

South Asia is no exception. There is no alternative to making peace and maintaining security whatever the price may be. I am confident that the distinguished participants in this workshop will demonstrate an ability to break old mental structures and infuse new thinking in our region. Only the ability for the courage to adapt to change will ensure the peaceful solution of disputes, and lay the foundation for the overall security and stability of South Asia.

The Government and the people of the Maldives will be happy to provide you a comfortable stay. I hope that the serenity of the sea around you will be a source of inspiration. I wish you the very best in your important work.

6

Simulation Exercises

SIMULATION exercises place participants in the position of conflict resolution managers and negotiators. We present two of the simulations presented by Mr William Weisberg at the Maldives workshop. The oil pricing simulation was used as an ice-breaker at the beginning of the workshop. The water resources simulation was based on a real conflict in South Asia. It was prepared by Mr Weisberg and Dr Jean Krasno.

Simulations are conducted by technical experts. It is recommended that professional experts be requested to explain and conduct the simulations given below.

There are three stages in the conduct of a simulation:
1. Instructions and explanation
2. The game
3. Debriefing and distilling of lessons.

The third stage is crucial. A professional facilitator would (1) ask the participants why they exercised certain options (2) draw lessons for negotiations and conflict management and (3) recommend strategies for negotiations in real life situations.

The simulations given below are only for the purpose of illustration. Professional experts can prepare simulations suitable for the objectives of a given workshop.

Oil Pricing Exercise
The facilitators should follow the instructions given below.

There are six teams: Alba 1, Batia 1, Alba 2, Batia 2, Alba 3, Batia 3. Alba 1 is engaged in conflict or cooperation with Batia 1. Alba 2 with Batia 2 and Alba 3 with Batia 3. When the game starts, it is assumed that there is hostile political and economic atmosphere under which each team has to operate. The atmosphere improves at a certain stage and again deteriorates at a further stage. Thus decision-making is attempted in different environments.

Instructions

1. Divide group into 3 Alba and 3 Batia Teams
2. Distribute Exercise Sheet
3. Explain: 8 rounds

    Profit will be cumulative

    3 Minutes for each bid preparation (time it)
4. Separate teams

   Ask them to read case

   A few minutes to discuss strategy in team
5. Round 1

   Explain: Up to 3 minutes to record secret price on paper.

    Results unknown until both bid.

   Bids exchanged

   Result recorded on tally sheet.
6. Round 2 and 3 same.
7. Before Round 4: Unusually favourable market.

    New pro-business administration

    Profit figures doubled this month.

    5 minute one-to-one meeting.

   Round 4, three minutes in team.
8. Round 5: climate back to same as 1-3.
9. Before Round 7: Great climate, Quadruple profit in 7 & 8

    1-to-1 conference again (not before 8)

   Round 7, three minutes to prepare
10. At end, allow 5 mins. in team to discuss decision-making in group.

Exercise Sheet

Alba and Batia are two less developed countries. Each produces oil at a cost of less than $10 per barrel. Their neighbouring country, Capita, is a land-locked, highly developed country that consumes a large amount of oil. Capita must buy all its oil from Alba or Batia unless it wants to pay an overland transportation charge of $25 per barrel.

Alba and Batia are each now selling oil to Capita at a price of $20 per barrel. So long as they both sell at the same price, each country can expect to retain about half of the Capita oil market. If one sells at a lower price than the other, it will expand the market share and increase its profits at the expense of the other. But neither can put the other permanently out of the oil business by undercutting other's price on sales to Capita.

You are a member of the Oil Pricing Board of Alba or Batia. Like other members of the Board, you were appointed by your country's Minister of Commerce and have eight months remaining in your current term of office. Each month the Board will be asked to set that month's price for your country's oil sales to Capita. Your goal as a Board is to maximize your country's profits on oil sales to Capita. Oil revenues are an important part of your country's Gross National Product. You are entirely indifferent to the oil profits of the other country.

Market research has demonstrated that the monthly profit for your country on oil sales to Capita will depend on the price you set and on the price set by the other country that sells oil to Capita. However, the possibility of overland delivery of oil from other producers makes it impossible to sell oil to Capita at a price of more than $30 per barrel.

By long-term agreement with Capita, the price that each country charges must be $10, $20 or $30. Historically, despite occasional short-term demand swings, the Capita oil market has been relatively stable, and the normal monthly profit that Alba and Batia can each expect to make on their oil sales to Capita is indicated in the following chart. The figures inside each box indicate the profit made during that month. The figure in the upper left of each box represents Alba's profit in millions of US dollars. The figure in the lower right of each box represents Batia's profits in millions of US dollars.

Price charged by Batia

		$ 30	$ 20	$ 10
Price charged by Alba	**$30**	A:$ 11 B:$ 11	A:$ 2 B:$ 18	A:$ 2 B:$ 15
	$20	A:$ 18 B:$ 2	A:$ 8 B:$ 8	A:$ 3 B:$ 15
	$10	A:$ 15 B:$ 2	A:$ 15 B:$ 3	A:$ 5 B:$ 5

Alba and Batia have a history of hostility and recently broke diplomatic relations. Hence each Board will have to set its price on the next month's sale of oil to Capita without knowing what price the other is going to charge. In the current volatile political climate (national elections in each country are only three months away), any attempt to confer with the other country would certainly result in your being dismissed from the Oil Pricing Board, and might result in your prosecution for treason.

Profit Record

Month	Price Chosen		Profit for Month		Cuml. Total Profit	
	Alba	*Batia*	*Alba*	*Batia*	*Alba*	*Batia*
1						
2						
3						
4						
5						
6						
7						
8						

Batia

Table letter:_____________

Month number:____________

Price:___________________

Batia

Table letter:_____________

Month number:____________

Price:___________________

Batia

Table letter:_____________

Month number:_____________

Price:_____________

Alba

Table letter:_____________

Month number:_____________

Price:_____________

Alba

Table letter:_____________

Month number:_____________

Price:_____________

Batia

Table letter:_____________

Month number:_____________

Price:_____________

Alba

Table letter:_____________

Month number:_____________

Price:_____________

Alba

Table letter:_____________

Month number:_____________

Price:_____________

De-briefing Questions
(by the facilitator to the players)

1.   (*a*) What did you see as your overall goal?
   (*b*) What was your overall strategy before the game began?
   (*c*) Why did you choose bid of X in Round 1?
2.   (*a*) What was your strategy in subsequent rounds?
   (*b*) How did it differ from your intended initial strategy?
   (*c*) What caused the changes?
3.   (*a*) Although there was no discussions prior to 6 rounds, was there a means of communication to other team?
   (*b*) What messages were you intending to signal to other team?
   (*c*) What message did you think you were receiving each time?
4.   (*a*) How did you handle decision-making within group?
   (*b*) How were disagreements handled?
   (*c*) Were you satisfied with the way your group worked together?
   (*d*) How would you work differently?
   (*e*) What would you recommend as a procedure?
5.   (*a*) How did you respond to breaches of trust by the other side?
   (*b*) What are the forces inducing competition or collaboration?

6. (*a*) What happened in the 1-to-1 conferences?
   (*b*) What was the agreement?
   (*c*) How firm was the commitment?
   (*d*) What were the pressures on the representatives?
7. How would your strategy change if the game were infinite?

Lessons

- Know your goal.
  This exercise emphasizes mid-term material gain.
  Goal is sometimes short-term, sometimes long-term.
  Goal is sometimes purely material, sometimes psychological (both).
  What works best under parameters of this exercise, might not in others.
- Know the other players' interests and perspective.
  Negotiation process and outcome are interactive.
  Outcome cannot be determined by one team alone.
  Environment will influence outcome (other team, sea of teams, norms, external pressures/market)
- Attend to level of perceptions.
  What is intended is not always what is heard. Often important to ask "what will be heard".
  Differing interests and experience will influence how an event is perceived. (e.g., was defection defensive or aggressive?)
- Future reality and even current climate are often uncertain.
  Trust or mistrust can establish environment of escalation or cooperation.
  Holding commitments helps to induce trust.
- Negotiation is a team sport.
  In negotiation, intra-level can be as influential as inter-group (and is often underestimated)
  Players rarely act unilaterally.
- Knowing above will allow you to be purposive, not reactive.
- In a mixed strategy environment, be clear, nice, provocable, and forgiving.

Water Resources

This simulation requires advance preparations. Then participants are divided into three country teams: Alpha, Gamma, Delta. Each team receives two sets of exercise sheets: one set describing the scenario which would be common to all teams and another set of confidential instructions separately for each time.

Instructions

1. Write out teams in advance.
2. Distribute material in advance
3. Give instructions
   - Features of the simulation
   - Parties
   - Issues (?)
   Questions?
4. Meet by country
   - Introduce yourselves. Develop your role.
   - Prepare strategy
   - Select a delegation
   Ancillary parties prepare alone
5. Negotiation Round #1
   - Those not in delegation, listen closely.
6. Debrief #1: preparation, interests, and building relationships.
7. Within country strategy session #2
   - Think about how to get an agreement
8. Negotiation Round #2
9. Debrief (#2): Finding a settlement and considerations in party negotiations.

Three-Nation Scenario

Three nations (Alpha, Gamma, Delta) make up an island continent in the Pacific Ocean. The terrain varies from high rugged mountains to rolling hills and delta lowlands. The climate is semi-tropical with mild temperatures in winter and a heavy rainy season for three months followed by a dry spell.

Alpha

Geography

- high, rugged mountains and some rich plateau land for agriculture;
- mountains hold the head waters for three major rivers;
- the coastline is very steep with high cliffs on the windward side of the island continent;
- there are no usable ports.

Assets

- water, tin, copper, nickel, wheat, coffee.

Gamma

Geography

- some high plateau with rolling hills, some lowland areas;
- coast is on the leeward side of the island continent;
- there are three major ports.

Assets

- good agriculture: wheat, rice, fruits, coffee; livestock; light and heavy industry; good ports for shipping industry and foreign trade; the largest and wealthiest of the three countries.

Delta

Geography

- lowlands and delta area with several important islands offshore;
- one major port.
- flooding is a major problem in the rainy season and silt deposited on the delta after monsoon is of very poor quality and has left some land unusable.
- the islands and coastline are very low and are in danger of erosion.

Assets

- agriculture: fruit, rice, truck gardens; offshore oil potential.

Regional Water Issues

Alpha's Hydroelectric Dam

- A dam for hydroelectric power is being proposed by Alpha. They plan to sell power to Gamma and Delta. The dam would affect the flow of water to those countries.

Gamma's Barrages

- Gamma has built two barrages on two rivers which divert the water supply away from Delta in the dry season. Gamma is accused of sending more water down towards Delta during monsoon. Flooding on delta of country Delta has got worse in last few years leaving poor quality silt.

Delta's Water Breaks

- Delta also fears rising water level and loss of land to erosion. Delta wants to build water breaks in the ocean, near its border with Gamma. Gamma is opposed to this because the water breaks might cause shoreline erosion along Gamma's coast.

Pollution

- The rivers are becoming polluted. Animal waste as well as industrial runoff contribute to a growing problem.

Scenario

Alpha wants to build a dam to produce power but doesn't have the assets to do it alone. It has appealed to the World Bank and the United Nations Development Program for financial support. Alpha has asked Gamma to invest but wants to maintain control of the dam.

Gamma has assets to invest and wants the power from the dam, but desires some control of the dam's operation. Local people in Gamma fear loss of water and have had major demonstrations in protest. Elections are coming up and the opposition party has taken up the issue. Talks between the two countries have broken down.

Delta fears the dam will cause less water to flow in the dry season and worse flooding in monsoon. They have complained to the UN and have asked the Secretary-General of the UN to intervene. He is sending a UN representative to meet the parties. They could use electric power, but don't have assets to buy it.

Alpha threatens to build the dam on its own with World Bank funding. Gamma announced it would send troops to stop the dam. Delta agreed to provide troops to Gamma.

All three countries are democracies with elected parliaments. Alpha is a presidential democracy with a president elected to a set term with elections held separately from the parliamentary elections. Gamma, the largest, is a constitutional monarchy with multi-party parliament and a coalition majority. The King retains policy-making powers but can be overruled by Parliament. Delta is a parliamentary democracy with a prime minister selected by the MPs as head of state. There are two major parties with a few smaller parties.

The regional security organization, Cooperative Association for Regional and Environmental Security (CARES) has called for a three-party round of talks on the crisis. The S-G's representative will attend the talks, along with a representative from the World Bank.

The three countries will first meet separately to prepare their strategies and select who will sit at the table.

Roles

Country Alpha	Country Gamma	Country Delta
President	King Prime Minister	Prime Minister
Foreign Minister	Foreign Minister	Foreign Minister
Defence Minister	Defence Minister	Defence Minister
Minister of Agriculture	Minister of Agriculture	Minister of Agriculture
Minister for Mining, Energy, and Natural Resources	Minister for Mining, Energy, and Natural Resources	Minister for Mining, Energy, and Natural Resources
MP Government Party	MP Government Party	MP Government Party
MP Opposition Party	MP Opposition Party MP third Party	MP Opposition Party MP third Party
Non-government Grass Roots Leader	Non-government Grass Roots Leader	Non-government Grass Roots Leader

International Actors

World Bank Official

Secretary General of regional organization: Cooperative Association for Regional and Environmental Security (CARES)

UN Secretary-General's Special Representative (UNDP official)

Confidential Instruction to Alpha

Alpha is very eager to see the proposed dam built. Our country has suffered a serious decline in economic activity in the past five years and a project the size of the Dam Project could provide the stimulus for a dramatic economic recovery. We need to begin substituting electric power for cooking and in some cases for heating and we need to provide electric power for industrial development.

Deforestation for the growing fuel needs of a growing population is causing major problems in soil erosion and land devastation. By controlling deforestation and the flow of water through the dam, we can limit flooding downstream of river during the rainy season. Through the creation of reservoirs behind the dam we can develop irrigation systems for our farmers during the dry season. With our growing population, we are finding it harder to feed our people.

We can also earn precious currency through the sale of electric power to our neighbours. We would like the cooperation of our neighbours but we want to control the operation of the dam to ensure our interests are met. If Gamma obtains significant control in return for investing in the dam, they will make sure that the dam only serves their interests, as they have done with other joint ventures in the past.

Delta has also objected to the dam project, but they are relatively weak and pose little concern to us. The major threat that they pose is not military or political, but that their own increasing poverty and agricultural problems are causing their people to cross our border and sap our very limited resources.

While the sale of power to our neighbours would be extremely beneficial to our economy, the overall importance of the project does not depend on that aspect, and we will build the dam without their help if we can secure the loan from the World Bank.

Confidential Instructions to Gamma

Our government is under pressure from our people living near the dam site and down the river not to allow the project to go through. With elections coming up in a few months, the major Opposition party has taken up the issue and claims that the dam will limit the amount of water in the dry season and open surges of water in the rainy season causing worse than normal flood damage.

The Opposition charges that the government has secretly agreed to take payoff money from Alpha to allow them to build the dam. The party in power acknowledges that electrical power would be a benefit to the region but cannot risk the political damage caused by agreeing to the project.

When Alpha claimed that it would go ahead with the project despite our country's objections, we had to demonstrate to our nation that we would take strong action. Therefore, we have threatened to send troops to stop the project.

Gamma would benefit from water management including flood control and irrigation in the dry season. But it is not clear that the dam would help or hurt water management. If the political problems could be overcome, Gamma would like to open a dialogue on the issue.

We might be willing to invest in the dam project in return for some control of the dam. This would serve two purposes. We could ensure that the dam was a benefit to our water management needs, and we could reassure our constituents living down the river that the dam would not be detrimental to their interests.

We have built two river barrages to provide a greater flow of water for our poorest constituents who live downstream. They have experienced deprivation and famine at times before the barrages were built, as it was difficult for them to maintain agricultural output for much of the year. Now, the barrages have increased the volume of water for their farming. We have been accused of intentionally sending more water toward the branch of the river that goes into Delta during flood season—which is untrue and insulting. Our engineers have suggested, though, that deforestation near the river has caused greater run-off during the rainy season, so the flow of water toward Delta might very well have increased over the years.

Confidential Instructions to Delta

Delta is very concerned about Alpha's proposed dam project. We are not in a position to buy the electric power that would be produced by the dam, so its construction does not seem to offer us any advantages. On the other hand, we are concerned that the dam will hold back the water in the dry season to fill Alpha's proposed reservoirs hurting Delta's farm industry. The dam would also release excess water in flood season causing damage. We are already experiencing heavy silt deposits after flood season and the dam could make it worse.

If the dam were to be built, we would want to have some control over its use. We might have some revenue available to purchase the needed electric power if we were to develop the off-shore oil potential. Right now, we do no have the resources to develop an oil industry, although studies have indicated that we might have substantial offshore oil deposits. We need to make our objections to the dam known. If it looks like the project will go ahead anyway, we want to gain some concessions from Alpha to help us with our economic development and water management needs.

We also have a dispute with Gamma over two barrages they have built to divert water in the dry season away from branches of the river which flow into Delta. We have also noticed that there is greater water volume down the river in rainy season, which is probably a result of Gamma's actions. If Gamma wants us to support their position we will demand that they remove the barrages. Why didn't they simply work with us to build reservoirs and storage tanks to manage water resources?

We intend to build some water breaks in the ocean near our border with Gamma. We need to stem the tides coming our way because our islands are only 1 meter above sea level, and there has been land erosion and damage to property on the islands.

Confidential Instructions to the Secretary-General of the Cooperative Association for Regional and Environmental Security (CARES)

You have organized this round of talks for the three regional players in this dispute because tensions have threatened security in the region. Your regional cooperation organization is devoted to increasing cooperation and diffusing conflict over security, environmental and economic development issues.

You will chair these discussions with the intention of helping the parties arrive at a settlement.

You do not want violence to break out over this dam issue because it would damage the reputation of the area in the eyes of the world community, it would be a disincentive for foreign investors, and might invite UN peacekeeping forces or other third party threats to regional sovereignty.

It would be helpful to demonstrate that CARES is capable of bringing this issue to a negotiated settlement. As the stature of CARES is enhanced, it can be more effective in locating opportunities for greater peace and cooperation in the area.

CARES was created with a mandate to deter outside aggression. It is more problematic to act as a deterrent to threats of aggression within the region, because the effectiveness of the organization depends on the goodwill of all the three countries involved in this conflict.

Prepare a strategy to help the parties reach agreement.

You will meet the UN and World Bank representatives prior to your meeting the delegations from Alpha, Gamma, and Delta.

Confidential Instructions for United Nations Secretary-General's Special Representative (UNDP official)

The Secretary-General is concerned about the growing tensions in this region, and has sent you to attempt to try to meet the parties to discuss their concerns and identify the causes of the dispute.

The UN Secretary-General would like the parties to know the UN is concerned about the region, and is not ignoring the issues. You should be sure to express the UN's interest.

The Secretary-General has sent a United Nations Development Programme official to these talks because your knowledge of water resources management should come in handy.

The UN Security Council members have made it clear that the Council is not in a position to send peace-keeping troops at this time, should this escalate into a military confrontation.

Your role is to help articulate the grievances of the parties and to try to facilitate progress toward a settlement. You probably should not take too forward a role in this because quiet diplomacy might be more effective in this conflict, and because the UN has little leverage to broker an agreement.

Review the scenario and develop a strategy that might facilitate agreement. You will first meet the World Bank and CARES representatives before attending a session with delegations from the three countries.

Confidential Instructions for World Bank Official

Alpha's recent application to build and operate a hydroelectric dam project is of great interest to the World Bank. We have not had a major project in this part of the globe in the history of the Bank and have been under some pressure to repair this omission. Unfortunately, some of our lower level staff appeared over-eager in the initial discussions with Alpha and left the impression that the Bank was ready to fund the project at very good terms without a careful study of the effects of the project on the environment and on the interests of the neighbouring countries.

The Bank believes that the production of electric power and control of the river for flood management and irrigation would support the economic development of the region as a whole. But, we will only fund the project if a system of water management can be worked out by the three countries. The agreement must be both environmentally sound and have the support of all three parties. Water management is a dynamic process and any agreement must look to the future by providing mechanisms for continual adjustments including a grievance review commission. The environmental aspects of the project are very important to the Bank because the World Bank has been severely criticized for ignoring the environmental impact of its projects in the past.

Our role is to facilitate such an agreement. The Bank will not fund the project unless these goals are met. You will have to determine whether the environmental concerns are addressed sufficiently by the agreement and whether the interests of the parties have been satisfied to the extent that the accord will hold up over time. You have flexibility within these constraints. You have the final responsibility to okay the loan.

Debriefing on Preparation, Interests, and Negotiating Relationships

1. What has transpired so far?
2. How did each party prepare?
   - Did you identify your own interests?
   - Did you try to identify the interest of other parties?
   - Did you determine your own opportunity costs?
   - Assess importance of on-going relationships, prioritizing, and considering how to enhance them? Who did this?
3. What were the negotiating strategies at the table?
   Was there discussion of interests or of positions?
4. What were the strategies for building good negotiating relationships?
   - With whom is good relationship most important?

Debriefing on Obtaining Settlement and Multi-party Negotiations

5. What factors influenced the outcome?
   - What appeared to facilitate forward motion?

- What appeared to be obstacles?
- (Note lack of agreement from different perspectives. Goal, vantage point makes something helpful to one and a hindrance to other.)

6. Obtaining a settlement
   - How did you attempt to do this?
   - Did you brainstorm options without committing?
7. Obstacles: What made agreement difficult? How did you handle it?
8. When you are working on regional or global cooperative effort, there are special issues in multilateral negotiations worth considering:

   (*a*) Must identify key stake holders.
   - Which parties should be at the table? (Extremist factions on each side?)
   - Which are necessary partners?
     What are the dimensions to take into account in deciding this?
     - Can you move forward without them?
     - When to bring them in? (Perhaps slowly build a coalition)

   (*b*) Two-table problem.
   Internal dynamics often receive too little attention. International community tends to see the conflict as two-party tension (ignores internal factions).
   - Must try to build internal consensus prior to negotiations
   - Build a rationale for constituents during and after
   - Be mindful of other parties' constituent constraints and how to overcome them.

   (*c*) Coalition-building
   - Did anyone try to build coalitions with particular partners?
   - Coalitions shift and can construct or block an agreement.
   - Must assess how to address blockers.

- Add issues to agenda to meet interests of blocking parties. (How? Example?)
- Third party can be useful.

9. How would settlement be reached?
   - Recommend a procedure (panel, delay general elections, etc.)
   - Build a relationship of mutual trust
   - Agree to a shared set of principles and concerns
   - Find an integrative solution.

7

Case Studies

CASE studies form an important part of an introductory conflict resolution workshop. They may also be used as reference points in an advanced level, substantive workshop.

We present three case studies in this section. Of them, the last one (parliamentary consensus in Sri Lanka) was presented by Mr Mangala Moonesinghe at the Maldives workshop. The other two are excerpted from an earlier publication of the ICPI.

The case studies by Mr Arthur Lall focus on direct negotiations between state parties to an international dispute.

The case study by Mr Inder Jit focuses on third party mediation in an internal conflict. Since all South Asian countries are plagued by internal conflicts, this may be useful.

The case study by Mr Mangala Moonesinghe examines an innovative instrument of parliament. This would be particularly useful for legislators.

In a Workshop, case studies are presented by experts. Sometimes the experts may have been directly involved in the conflict resolution process covered by the case study. Sometimes they may be scholars. The case studies may be from the region or outside. The main purpose of presenting case study is to distill lessons and provide reference points for the conflict under consideration.

CASE STUDY
SUEZ AND VIETNAM TALKS
Arthur Lall

If peace is to serve as the basis of the New World order at a practical level, negotiations must commence to establish new institutions of governance in various regions. There is a distinction between ordinary diplomatic negotiation and negotiations for peace. When you are negotiating for peace, you are trying to avoid a major conflict of a war. Avoidance of war is a very serious business. If you are negotiating for trade, transit, cultural or communication matters, it is a different thing altogether. When negotiations take place for peace, there is normally a greater sense of responsibility among negotiators than those engaged in other negotiations because they have a greater sense of burden, or tasks they are facing.

When President Nasser of Egypt nationalized the Suez Canal Company in 1956, there was an uproar in the Western world, particularly in France and Britain—the two countries which virtually owned the Suez Canal. They said that it was a complete breach of faith. But President Nasser insisted that he only had nationalized the Suez Canal Company and the canal itself had already been a part of Egypt. But the uproar was so great that a conflict seemed imminent. And negotiations to avoid that conflict were called for.

Sir Anthony Eden, the British Prime Minister, who was a sick man, called for a conference in London in the early part of summer of 1956 to try and find a solution. It was primarily a conference of major users. Even though smaller users such as India and Sri Lanka were present, the Western powers were the major participants at the conference. The Soviet Union played a minor role. It was in a sense an unbalanced conference because it was highly dominated by the West. Egypt itself was not present at the conference, which created a further problem to find a solution. India acted as a proxy for Egypt. We kept very closely in contact with Mr Ali Sabri, President Nasser's personal envoy.

The difficulties presented by Egypt's absence show that it is not possible to find a solution to a conflict unless all the aggrieved parties participate in the negotiations.

India presented a solution in the form of an Advisory Council which would be consulted on the working of the canal. But Britain and France insisted on an arrangement in which they would have an authority to maintain and run the canal.

State of Balance

In trying to negotiate for peace, there should not be complete imbalance among the parties involved. Here there was an imbalance in the sense that Egypt was not present and Mr Dulles thought it necessary to throw the weight of the US behind UK and France. The negotiating tables were structured in favour of one side. It was naturally difficult to find a solution acceptable to all sides.

Let me illustrate my point with another example—that of Vietnam negotiations in Paris in the mid-1960s. The Americans were very reluctant to enter into any negotiations with North Vietnam. The result was that a war went on in Vietnam. Finally the US agreed to allow North Vietnam to be present at the conference but they absolutely refused to allow Vietcong, the militant opposition within South Vietnam, to come to the negotiating table. Finally after a year, the US had to give in.

It means that the greatest power in the world, the United States, had to sit at the conference table on the same level not only with North Vietnam but also Vietcong. This is a very important point. It establishes that, contrary to a routine view, you cannot get peace by negotiating from a position of pure strength. You get negotiations only when, no matter how powerful one party is, for the purpose of negotiations all parties are ready to sit down as equals. It is awfully difficult for great powers to divest themselves of their position of strength. It was obviously difficult for the United States to agree to Vietcong, North Vietnam and so on to be present at a conference table on an equal basis. But they had to do it in order to make negotiations for peace possible.

India is relatively powerful in South Asia. Therefore there is clearly an imbalance between India and her neighbouring countries. If India were to settle an issue with neighbours purely on the basis of strength, the weak neighbours might accept India's decision for a short while. In the long-run, resistance builds up and after a few years, the small country finds some opportunity, or some excuse to reassert itself. That is precisely what happened in the case of Nepal.

In short, to negotiate for peace, the following rules must be followed:

1. All parties to the conflict should be represented at the negotiating table.
2. There should be a balance of power at negotiations.
3. All parties involved in negotiations should treat each other with equality.

When you arrive at such a situation, negotiations are possible. Psychologically a situation is created where all parties realize that they must be prepared to give and take. They can look at each other in the eyes and talk business. That is what negotiations are.

In the case of the war between Iraq and Iran, one party attacked the other because it was stronger than the other. The other party reacted. Finally, when both parties realized, through a military stalemate, that they were in a state of balance, they began to negotiate. This is the worst way of arriving at a state of balance, namely through actual war. The point is that when parties are at balance of power, they come to negotiating tables. These negotiations are bound to be prolonged. But when they arrive at a solution, that will be a much different situation than say, the Treaty of Versailles of 1919, when defeated Germany was simply dictated to by victorious France and Great Britain. This kind of peace treaty is very fragile. In the case of Iran-Iraq, it was not a victorious party dictating to a defeated party. They negotiated as equals and that is why their truce might be a lasting one. The Treaty of Versailles created a situation which led to World War Two.

(From *The New World Order*, ed. Sundeep Waslekar, Konark, 1991)

CASE STUDY
INDIA'S GORKHA PROBLEM
Inder Jit

It is generally conceded that resolving ethnic conflicts in most parts of the world is quite difficult. But it is necessary to bear in mind that there have also been success stories in resolving ethnopolitical conflicts in South Asia in recent years. The question is whether we can draw any lessons from these success stories and apply them to address the outstanding issues.

The peaceful resolution of the 80-year old Gorkhaland conflict in India is one of the most striking examples of how even a private citizen can contribute to end a serious problem with a right combination of will, approach, skill and determination. It would be useful to take an overview of the history of this problem before I present a case study of how it was resolved.

The Nepali-speaking Gorkha community is dispersed all over India but its largest concentration is in the Darjeeling hill area in the north-east. From an administrative point of view the hills are a part of West Bengal state. This state was divided in 1947 when its eastern wing became Pakistan which in 1971 became Bangladesh. Ever since the beginning of the 20th century the Gorkhas have been averse to be administered by Bengal (until 1947) or West Bengal (since 1947). They had submitted memoranda to the British government in 1907, 1917, 1929 and 1935 asking for a separate Darjeeling district administrative unit outside of Bengal province. The All India Gorkha League, formed in 1943 just before India became independent, also made similar pleas to governments in New Delhi in 1952, 1956, 1970 and 1981 for a separate statehood from West Bengal. The Gorkha statehood movement received a special impetus in the early 1980s with the emergence of Mr Subhash Ghising, soldier-turned-author of 20 books, who launched the Gorkha National Liberation Front (GNLF) in 1980. He instantly obtained massive support from the Nepali-speaking Indians at the grass-root level.

Causes of Conflict

That the Gorkhas, particularly the youth, desperately looked for a firebrand and charismatic leader like Mr Ghising to press for this demand of separate statehood can be understood if the conditions in which these people have been living are appreciated. Darjeeling is a popular hill resort not only of Bengal but also of India. But municipal services are in a shambles. There is an acute shortage of water and power. Roads have fallen to pieces. You even find yourself walking on underground pipes! Tourism is on the decline. The locals have few opportunities for either jobs or in education. I had visited Darjeeling in 1964 and I was again there in 1986 and I could notice the deterioration of this strategic district of West Bengal over the last 20 years.

Apart from the economic problems, the Gorkhas also have an identity problem. They are treated as foreigners (Nepalese) and not Indians on account of their language and physical features. Discrimination, repression and petty politics by West Bengal politicians had convinced them that the only solution to their problem was an independent state.

I met Mr Ghising purely accidentally in May 1986 when I was visiting Darjeeling on a personal holiday. It was a time when the Gorkha agitation was at its height with a highly successful boycott of administrative and economic activities. It seemed to be set to take a violent turn, particularly since Mr Ghising had announced his decision to launch an agitation on Independence day (August 15).

Mr Ghising made it clear to me that he wanted independent statehood for the Gorkhas within the federal framework of India. He did not in any way advocate break-up from India even though he had once raised the issue in letters addressed to the Secretary-General of the United Nations and Heads of foreign Governments. All he was demanding was a power for the people at the grass-root level as it had been given to some other groups in India. I could appreciate his demand since political power for economic decision-making is necessary in India where the political system clearly commands the economic system. I urged him to find a peaceful answer to his grievances since violence would further deteriorate the local economy.

Solution

A few days later Mr Ghising suddenly called on me at my New Delhi residence and sought my help in finding a peaceful solution to the Gorkha problem. He had approached me on two counts. He was convinced of my impartial attitude due to my objective press reporting of my meeting with him. He had also heard of my access to the highest echelons of the political leadership.

I approached Mr Rajiv Gandhi, then Prime Minister of India, and his cabinet colleagues who asked me to convince them of Mr Ghising's not being anti-national through a concrete course of action. Mr Ghising responded to my request by cancelling the Independence Day agitation. This success facilitated involvement of the West Bengal provincial government in our efforts to find a peaceful solution to the problem.

The state government was not obviously willing to accept the creation of an independent Gorkhaland. Bengal had been divided in 1947 amidst massive violence and a second partition of the state would have invited even more annihilation. But the leaders of the state as well as the central government were willing to accept a solution which would give powers to the Gorkha people to run their own life without splitting the state or the country. I therefore designed the concept of a Hill Council which would be within the overall jurisdiction of Bengal but which would enjoy administrative power on several local matters.

This solution meant going more than half way to meet Mr Ghising's demand for statehood and the establishment's intransigence with regard to devolution of power. I could see the theory of linkages between peace and development being operational here as I convinced Mr Ghising to accept a semi-state and start the development process rather than waiting for a full-fledged state and increasing destruction.

Secondly, I persuaded the West Bengal state government to seek a political solution, and not a police solution as the latter would incite violence.

Once both sides thus saw sense in peace, it was a matter of few technicalities which the bureaucrats took their own time in sorting out before we finally signed the Darjeeling accord creating a Hill Council in 1988.

It was the first time that a private citizen had played a role in defusing an explosive situation. The success of the Gorkha accord also inspired the then President Ershad of the neighbouring Bangladesh to solve the problem of Chakma tribals in Chittagong Hill tract. President Ershad, in fact, went a step further by according the Chittagong Hill Council not only administrative powers but also basic police powers.

Lessons from the Accord

What lessons can we draw from the success of the Gorkha accord which is one of the few accords not to backfire among all accords for communal and ethnic peace signed in India in the 1980s.

One, it is important to realize that people of India, as in other developing countries, are increasingly demanding political powers to manage their own affairs. This is an inevitable political process and the response to it must be essentially political, not police action. The latter convinces the agitating people even more of the need to have governing powers and can lead to fruitless violence.

Secondly, I had no personal axe to grind as a mediator. I could, therefore, provide total confidence and trust to all parties to the conflict.

Thirdly, I always placed all my cards on the table against the standard practice not to reveal all your cards while you are bargaining. I used a different approach. I was very open, demonstrating that I was not a broker. I was an intermediary. There is a difference between brokers and intermediaries.

We cannot solve Punjab and other problems because there are too many brokers but no intermediaries.

Fourthly, it is important to have a dialogue. Many times it is a question of being able to communicate properly in these kinds of negotiations. We should remember that everybody wants a reasonable settlement. Nobody wants to abet killing for the sake of killing. The difference is always about the ways to accomplish a particular objective. You can solve many a problem by putting across your position in the right manner. For example, Mr Ghising's letters to the Heads of foreign Governments raised doubts about his intentions. But his appropriately worded statement of commitment to India on Independence Day brought all parties to the negotiating table.

Fifthly, persistence is important. Many times I thought that I was hitting my head against a hard wall as the government leaders were occupied with other problems and could not respond to Mr Ghising's gestures. If we had therefore left the efforts half way, we would have witnessed more violence and destruction.

The GNLF put the final seal on the solution in late 1988 when they asked me, a non-Gorkha, to contest an election and represent their interests in the Parliament. My victory demonstrates the GNLF commitment to the Indian nation. More important, it proves that a peaceful solution attracts everyone. It also establishes supremacy of dialogue over street violence in addressing internal grievances in developing nations.

(From *The New World Order*, ed. Sundeep Waslekar, Konark, 1991)

CASE STUDY
PEACE BY PARLIAMENTARY CONSENSUS IN SRI LANKA
Mangala Moonesinghe

The population of Sri Lanka is 17 million. The major communities are the Sinhalese, constituting 75 per cent of the population and the Sri Lankan Tamils forming 12.5 per cent. The Sinhalese are Buddhists and are descendants of migrants from the north of India around the 5th century BC. This is buttressed by empirical evidence of linguistic and cultural ties with northern India. The ancestors of the Sri Lankan Tamils are those who remained in the country consequent on military expeditions and other social movements between South India and Sri Lanka. The Muslims who make up 7 per cent of the population claim their ancestry to Arab traders of the early period. The Plantation Tamils who total 5 per cent of the population were brought by the British to work on the tea plantations and are concentrated in the central hills.

The on-going conflict is between the Sri Lanka Tamils and the Sinhala leadership. The differences between the two communities polarized after 1956 when Sinhala was made the official language. Agitation by the Tamil politicians for parity of status in language remained unanswered for over 35 years. As time passed, naturally more demands were made by the Tamil leadership. Today, many of the grievances have been addressed and Sinhala and Tamil are the official languages with English as the national language. On August 3, 1995 a far-reaching package of devolution for the Tamils was introduced by the Sri Lankan President, Ms Chandrika Kumaratunga. The proposals for devolution are an elaboration of an earlier agreement on some intractable ethnicity-related issues by the former government and a majority of the Opposition parties in Parliament through the process of the Parliamentary Select Committee.

Historic Agreement on the Ethnic Question by the Government and the Majority Parliamentary Opposition

The importance of the 1993 agreement in the Parliamentary Select Committee is the consensus arrived at between the Government and the Sri Lanka Freedom Party, the main Opposition in Parliament, for the first time in the history of the country on the ethnic issues. In 1958, an understanding between Mr S.W.R.D. Bandaranaike, the Prime Minister and Mr Chelvanayagam, leader of the Tamil Parties, failed to be implemented as it was sabotaged by the Opposition United National Party. In 1966, an attempt to reconcile issues between the United National Party Government and the Tamil political parties was rejected by the Sri Lanka Freedom Party in Opposition.

Since then, the 1993 Parliamentary Select Committee agreement between the United National Party Government and the Sri Lanka Freedom Party and other Opposition parties has become a landmark in the ethnic agenda. The agreement was presented to Parliament and accepted without dissent. Such a consensus between the main political parties to take certain crucial national issues outside the narrow confines of political competition should be emulated by countries in the region and elsewhere.

Pre-condition for Consensus in the Parliamentary Select Committee of 1993

There are many factors that combine to form the agenda for such an endorsement:-

(*i*) The person who initiates such a move should be seen as a person of integrity, and acceptable to all shades of political opinion. He must be looked upon by the other political parties as a Member of Parliament who has attempted to rise above petty political considerations at all times. He must have a record in Parliament and outside as a person whose criticisms of other political parties were on a fair assessment of policy only and not for parochial or political considerations. He must be associated in Parliament or outside as accepting and commending publicly the policies of other political parties when it was felt to be the outcome of diligently considered opinion. It must be clear that the person who initiates a proposal on a national issue has no hidden agenda of seeking an undue advantage for any political party.

(*ii*) The convener of a controversial national issue seeking reconciliation through political consensus must contact extremists' opinion on both sides of the divide and attempt a compromise that contains some common ground acceptable to both ends of the spectrum. In doing so, it is useful to point out to intransigent opinion, the futility of all concerned parties continuing to maintain an intractable position. This is mandatory as the extremists' opinion is always the most vocal.

(*iii*) It is prudent not to initially present to one's own party the opportunity to discuss and obtain permission to commence a move to resolve an acrimonious national conflict, as considerations within one's own party can block any further progress. One must be conscious of the fact that those opposing such a move in the party would be few, but articulate. A silent majority in the party will approve, though they will not go out of the way to risk their necks, a matter which is not seen as of immediate personal gain to them, and particularly, when the outcome of the success of the whole exercise is in the realm of uncertainty. Therefore having skirted one's own party apparatus, assessed opinions, and when fairly convinced that one is on firm ground, it is better to go public, knowing the time is opportune for wide approval. The party is then confronted with a *fait accompli*. On the demonstration of public goodwill the inner party battle is over, provided some background work is undertaken on winning party stalwarts.

(*iv*) There are many issues that affect the national constituency marginally. Taking up their cause is a risk. But if emotional issues affecting human life and hindering national progress, such as a violent conflict between communities and the nation, are highlighted, public applause is assured, particularly if the conflict has gone on for a long time with the sacrifice of many lives and without an end in sight. The longer the duration of the crisis and the greater the cost in lives and material, the greater the chance of success for the peace initiative. Violent human conflict in its nascent stage may be devoid of public acceptance until it endures for some time without a chance of termination in sight and at tremendous loss of life. Then the time will be opportune for an attempt at peace.

(*v*) The wording of the motion or the terms of reference for peace must be carefully done in order to display no bias to either of the protagonists. This is of utmost value if initially mass consensus is sought, for example, I quote the wording of the motion placed in Parliament which created the Parliamentary Select Committee—"That this Parliament is of opinion that a Select Committee of Parliament be appointed—

(*a*) to arrive at a political solution to the question involving the devolution of power to the northern and eastern provinces;

(*b*) to prevent—

(*i*) the disintegration of the nation;

(*ii*) the killings of innocent civilians, members of the armed forces and the youth fighting for a cause;

(*iii*) the increased militarization of the culture of violence in our country.

(*c*) to achieve peace and political stability and utilize the reduced defence expenditure for rapid economic growth and national development.

It will be observed that the use of the words "youth fighting for a cause" won the sympathy of the whole range of Tamil opinion. If words such as "Tamil terrorists" had been used instead, the motion would appear to have pronounced a value judgement. Almost all abhor violence, and national development has a stake for all.

(*vi*) When a motion is moved in Parliament, as in the case of Sri Lanka under specific days allotted for private Members' motions, and if, as mentioned earlier there is an atmosphere of welcome by the public, then all parties are likely to vote for it to be on the bandwagon, as nobody previously dared to bell the cat. But soon the initial public enthusiasm will begin to sag as other events overtake the issue, making the work of the committee stable. This would also happen to an extra-parliamentary body appointed to negotiate. It is natural that often the media and publicity grabbing politicians and individuals will commence sniping and pointing out actual and imaginary defects in the peace process. Antagonistic opinions will surface and become more vocal. It is essential then to remain silent and demonstrate extreme patience. Attempts to contradict criticisms by these groups will only help to prolong their adverse comments and keep alive an inconvenient debate.

(*vii*) Apart from the formal meetings of the Parliamentary Select Committee or the negotiations, it is important to resort to behind-the-scenes diplomacy. Informal meetings with those directly involved in the issues or their surrogates is mandatory. At times it will appear to be useful to pick the more flexible and reasonable members of the opposite group of negotiators and continue the informal dialogue. Even in your own side it is necessary to use members who are more supportive of consensual resolution by informal and friendly discussions with them, in order to utilize them to persuade the more difficult members.

(*viii*) When a breakthrough is in sight, snatch the opportunity, close the sessions temporarily and consolidate the achievements.

(*ix*) If the negotiations are incomplete, either fix another date or place the matters agreed upon, for the specifics to be worked out by a technical committee appointed by both sides. This creates an impression, that an expert team is non-political and is bound to apply tried scientific formulae with cold detachment.

This is the methodology that was used in arriving at a Parliamentary consensus between the Government and the major Opposition parties over the ethnic question in Sri Lanka. This is the first time there was agreement to change the Constitution from a unitary to a federal one, a highly inflammable issue. The word 'Federal' was not applied. Instead the Committee recommended to Parliament to adopt a Constitution on lines similar to the Indian Constitution. The committee also recommended the elimination of the Concurrent list and the devolution of the subjects to the Provinces. It did not settle the conflict, but it started a process for peace.

Results of the Parliamentary Select Committee of 1993

Free and fair elections were held in a large part of the war-ravaged area on the recommendations of the Parliamentary Select Committee. The present proposals presented by President Kumaratunga contain much of the basic ground covered by the Parliamentary Select Committee. It has been stated by the Minister of Constitutional Affairs, who was mainly responsible for the present proposal, that they are an elaboration of the agreement of the Parliamentary Select Committee.

PART II

SOUTH ASIA

8

Conflicts in South Asia

THE purpose of this section is to provide a summary of conflicts in South Asia and efforts made to resolve them. It gives a list of conflicts resolved as well as those which are outstanding—at the beginning of 1996.

The list of 'conflicts yet to be resolved' would be useful to identify specific conflicts to be addressed in a workshop or a political process.

The list of 'conflicts resolved' would be useful to identify case studies which can be taken up for discussion.

The long list of 'conflicts resolved' should assure participants that conflict resolution is a feasible proposition in South Asia.

Conflicts between India and Pakistan

Conflicts Resolved

- In April 1950, India and Pakistan signed a pact on the treatment of religious minorities in their respective countries.
- In 1960 the two countries settled five disputed claims along the then West Pakistan-India border.
- The Simla conference in June 1972 attempted to construct a post-war order for the region. Agreement reached on these issues—normalizing diplomatic relations, resuming trade, communication, travel, and fixing a line of control

in Kashmir.
- Tripartite agreement on Pakistan's prisoner of war issue settled in April 1974.
- Division of assets and liabilities. It was decided in December 1947 that the Government of Pakistan would receive 750 million rupees from India as its share of the balances in undivided India.
- River water dispute. The Indus water treaty signed in September 1960.
- Rann of Kutch boundary dispute. Resolved by a three-member commission in Geneva in 1968.
- Salal Dam Agreement. Signed in 1978.

Conflicts yet to be Resolved
- **Kashmir.** It is the only major outstanding unresolved dispute between India and Pakistan since 1947. The matter has been on the UN agenda since 1948. India and Pakistan have fought two wars over Kashmir and the recent deterioration in relations between New Delhi and Islamabad is related to an uprising in the Indian-controlled part of Kashmir.
- **Siachen.** Since 1984, India and Pakistan have been militarily engaged over the Siachen Glacier. Historically, the agreement of 27 July 1949 that defined the cease-fire line between India and Pakistan in Kashmir, left its northern end vague. In the Simla Agreement, a line of control was drawn up afresh and defined on 12 November 1972, but it did not extend to the Siachen Glacier. In 1984 the race for control over Siachen began between India and Pakistan. In June 1989, on the occasion of the fifth round of the Indo-Pakistan defence secretaries' talks, the two countries were close to an agreement on Siachen. They had agreed to work towards a comprehensive settlement based on redeployment of their forces to reduce the chances of conflict, avoidance of the use of force, and the determination of future positions on the ground so as to conform to the Simla Agreement and to ensure a durable peace in the

Siachen area. But, according to Pakistan, India backed out of the understanding it had reached with Islamabad in June 1989. Since then no breakthrough has been achieved on the settlement of the Siachen dispute.

- **Nuclear Issue**. The Indo-Pakistan disagreement on the question of nuclear non-proliferation in South Asia not only concerns New Delhi and Islamabad but also external powers. India has termed the Nuclear Non-Proliferation Treaty (NPT) of 1968 discriminatory and has refused to sign it and has called for the inclusion of China for any sort of understanding on the nuclear issue. Pakistan has made it clear that it will not unilaterally sign the NPT unless India does the same.

- **Wuler Barrage**. The Wuler Barrage dispute concerns a barrage to be constructed by the Indian Government on the Jhelum River below the Wuler Lake in order to improve the lake's navigability during the winter when there is a drop in the water level. New Delhi launched the Tulbul Navigation Project to regulate the decrease of water. The Jhelum is one of three rivers that the Indus Treaty of 1960 (signed by India and Pakistan) assigns to Pakistan for unrestricted use, but with precise exceptions. One of them is "any control or use of water for navigation" by India provided it has not diminished the volume of water. Storage of water or construction of storage works is forbidden. The issue, therefore, is whether the barrage on river Jhelum will be a project for the "control or use of water for navigation" or is a "storage work." Since the waters will be confined for some time in order to raise the level of the Wuler Lake, there will be "storage temporarily." India has shown concern for the lower riparian (Pakistan) and suspended work on the project. Talks on the Wuler Barrage are continuing between New Delhi and Islamabad. Pakistan wants certain safeguards from India that the volume of water in the Jhelum river as it enters Pakistan will not be diminished and that the Wuler Barrage project will be in the interest of both India and Pakistan.

- **Demarcation of Sir Creek**. Sir Creek is a 60-mile long estuary in the marshes of the Rann of Kutch. The Indo-Pakistan Western Boundary Case Tribunal's Award signed on 19 February 1968, apart from settling the Rann of Kutch dispute, did not demarcate the boundary from the top of Sir Creek westward to north of the Creek on the Arabian Sea. The Tribunal noted that "in view of the aforesaid agreement, the question concerning the Sir Creek part of the boundary is left out of consideration." It has now become a bone of contention between India and Pakistan. India contends that the boundary lies in the middle of the Creek. Pakistan claims that it lies on its eastern bank on the Indian side and therefore, the entire Creek belongs to Pakistan. Pakistan insists that the creek boundary be delimited first so as to establish the point on land from which the sea boundary is to be limited. India's concerns centre on the maritime boundary. The Sir Creek dispute is included in Indo-Pakistan parleys to settle conflicts, but no breakthrough has been achieved so far.

Conflicts between India and Bangladesh

Conflict Resolved

Handing over Tin Bigha corridor to Bangladesh. India has handed over the enclave in what can be termed as a major diplomatic victory. Realignment of the border is over and the issue is resolved.

Conflicts yet to be Resolved

- **Ganga Water Dispute**. The Indian government says that Bangladesh's share of the Ganga's water will progressively decline because of the increasing demand of river water in the upper reaches. It advises Bangladesh to accept an agreement on the Brahmaputra's water instead.

  But Bangladesh says it has an inalienable claim to the sharing of water from the Ganga as the lower riparian country. Besides, it refuses to settle for a share of only one international river when it has a claim on the Ganga water too.

- **Chakma Refugees**. The first and second phase of repatriation of Chakma refugees in year 1989 and 1992 was successful. However, India wants the rest of the 56,000 Chakma refugees mostly settled in the North-East, to be repatriated. It also wants the Bangladesh government to provide land to them, since the land and the houses have been taken over by the Muslims and the security forces.

- **New Moore Island**. New Moore island is only 5.2 kms away from the Indian land boundary and quite far removed from the nearest point on Bangladesh territory. The island emerges at the estuary of the border river Harrabhanga when it separates India and Bangladesh. Bangladesh was not even aware of the existence of the island until 1974 when it was brought to their notice by India. Bangladesh laid their claim only in 1979 while India thinks the island belongs to it.

Conflicts between India and Nepal

Conflict Resolved

- For various reasons, political and historical, India is perceived in Nepal as the big brother. This feeling was reinforced after India reduced entry points for goods heading for Nepal in 1989, resulting in shortages of just about all essential items and commodities in the Himalayan kingdom. This created serious problems for the Nepalese. While the ostensible reason for the restriction on the number of entry into Nepal was that a new transit treaty had not been signed, the row was actually sparked off following Nepalese attempts to buy arms from China.

  The problem was resolved when Nepalese Congress was voted to power in the first democratic election in Nepal in 1990. In December 1990 the new transit treaty was signed.

Conflicts yet to be Resolved

- **Treaty of 1950**. Nepal wishes to end the tilt towards India and balance it with China. It does not want what it calls 'Indian Security Umbrella' as provided for in the 1950 Friendship Treaty. It wants to renew it. Nepal says that the treaty violates Nepal's sovereign status, specially Article 5 which makes it mandatory for Nepal to inform India about any arms purchase. On the other hand, Indian government maintains that the treaty provides certain privileges for Nepalese residing in India. For instance, Nepalese residing in India get the same facilities as Indians regarding the ownership of property, while Indians do not enjoy similar privileges in Nepal. Moreover, the treaty provides Nepal with trade and transit rights with minimum duty payment. The Indian government feels that should the treaty be scraped Nepal will be the bigger looser.

- **The Tanakpur Accord** was signed by Nepal's former prime minister Mr G.P. Koirala. The Adhikari government called it an unequal accord on sharing of the water of the river Mahakali, alleging that G.P. Koirala government had sold Nepal's right in return for a small share of power to be generated by the project. The Adhikari government had all along maintained that the accord should be renegotiated. The coalition government which came to power after the fall of the Adhikari government in late 1995 had not articulated a clear stand on the issue. The Indian government maintains that the accord was signed between the heads of the states and should be maintained in accordance with International law. Nepal also wants 2 MW of power generated from the project free of charge.

- **Sharada River Treaty**. This treaty was signed in 1920 by the then Rana of Nepal and the representative of British India. Nepal feels that this treaty is redundant.

Sharada river flows from Nepal but from time to time it zigzags into the Indian territory due to which the treaty was signed, giving India 80,000 cusecs of water and Nepal 3,000 cusecs of water. In terms of water resources in the world, Nepal is among the richest and in summer months Northern states in India face water problem. Nepal wants 1000 cusecs of water more which it could get from other project.

Conflicts between India and Sri Lanka

Conflicts Resolved

- Agreement on stateless people was reached by Prime Minister L.B. Shastri and Mrs S. Bandaranaike in October 1964. The Agreement provided for the settlement of 8,75,000 persons—3,00,000 to be granted Sri Lankan citizenship and 5,25,000 to be repatriated to India within a period of 15 years. The 'Status and Future' of the remaining 1,50,000 would be settled under a separate agreement. During Mrs Gandhi's visit to Sri Lanka in September 1967, it was agreed that the case of residual number of 1,15,000 persons would be taken up after the major part of the 1964 agreement was implemented. A settlement of this problem was reached only in 1973 during Mrs Gandhi's second visit to Sri Lanka.
  It was agreed that an increase of 10 per cent each year over the initial figure of 35,000 mentioned in the 1964 Agreement would be made. In the following year, agreement on the final phase of the issue was concluded when Mrs S. Bandaranaike visited India. This concerned the fate of the remaining 1,50,000. Both the countries agreed to accept half of the total number each.
- Agreement on 1979 to decide the jurisdiction of Kuchchativu island in favour of Sri Lanka.

Conflicts yet to be Resolved

- No direct conflict. Various Sri Lankan governments have had different views on India's possible role in Sri Lanka's internal conflict in the North-East where Tamil groups have launched an agitation for independence.

Conflicts between Nepal and Bhutan

- They have only one conflict so far and it has to be resolved.

Conflict yet to be Resolved

- **Refugees and Separatist Conflict**. People of Nepalese origin in Bhutan's southern district of Samchi, Sarbhang, and Samdrap Jongkh have, for the past five years, been engaged in militant movement demanding greater political and cultural freedom. Some of the militants even nurture the notion of Gorkhaland, a territory that would include parts of India, Nepal and Bhutan.

  None of this is acceptable to Bhutan, which says that the agitationists are not bonafide citizens of the country. Bhutan is not happy with the role of Nepalese government in the Movement, particularly Nepal's request that Bhutan must take back the 80,000 Bhutanese refugees of Nepalese origin, who obviously sympathize with the separatist movement, camping in the southern part of Nepal. King Wangchuck says that he will take back only those who are bonafide Bhutanese citizens and had fled in panic or under pressure from the militants.

  As a result of this, now nearly 1,25,000 refugees are staying in North Bengal with the help of UNHCR and few in the Eastern district of Nepal.

Regional Effort for Conflict Resolution

- Efforts to promote regional conflicts resolution and cooperation began in March 1947 when the Indian Council of World Affairs convened the first 'Asian Relation Conference'. The conference hosted 25 Asian nations, discussed problems related to colonialism, racism, migration and cooperation in agriculture and industry.

- Colombo conference, April 1954, December 1954, December 1956 to discuss an agenda including colonialism, the hydrogen bomb, communism and economic cooperation.

- Bandung, April 1955, despite disagreement on condemning communist expansion there was agreement to cooperate in economic and cultural areas.

- November 1956, Colombo powers met to discuss the Hungarian crisis and Suez crisis.
- Effort to launch regional cooperation advanced by Mr Zia-ur Rahman who formally proposed it in 1980, modest cooperation in functional area, began in 1985 as SAARC.
- India-Pakistan talks at the 1986 summit apparently played a mellowing role in the 1986-87 exercise crisis.

External Efforts for Conflict Resolution

- **Britain**: From 1946 to the early 1960's, Britain's policies after partition were directed towards preserving the strategic unity of the sub-continent. The initial British plan involved a joint defence council, covering financial and economic matters, communications and foreign policy. The plan failed because of the 1948 war. The British cooperation was restricted to bring about UN-sponsored solution to Kashmir and mediation in the Kutch in 1965.
- **Iran**. From 1969 to 1979, attempted to bring India and Pakistan closer in extended version of regional cooperation for development.
- **The US and USSR**. During 1952-59 the US had formal alliance relationship with Pakistan; with India there were informal arrangements and economic aid programme; UK and US helped India with arms during the China war. US tried to encourage India and Pakistan to settle their differences and engage in regional cooperation and negotiations over Kashmir.

   The Soviet Union brokered agreement at Tashkent in 1966 between India and Pakistan ending confrontation. In 1969 USSR proposed Asian security pact, rejected by Pakistan, which felt it was anti-Chinese. In 1971 Treaty of Friendship was entered between India and USSR.

   After Soviets withdrew from Afghanistan they made it clear that they would not support India in the Kashmir crisis. The US and Russia are engaged in regular consultation over South Asia and both sides are cooperating in resolving the Kashmir crisis.

9

Conflict Resolution Projects in South Asia

T HE objective of this chapter is to provide a list of non-governmental conflict resolution projects undertaken in South Asia in the 1990s.

This list would be useful in designing follow-up processes at a workshop.

—Certain ideas which are already being implemented may not be repeated to avoid duplication.

—Certain ideas may be good but they may not be effectively implemented by non-political bodies. They would get upgraded if they are adapted by political parties and parliamentary institutions.

—Certain ideas may be good in essence but weak in structure. It may be possible to adapt them with structural improvement.

—Institutions and persons involved in pursuing some of the projects can be tapped as resources for published information and live presentations.

—Some projects may be candidates for collaborative efforts as non-political institutions can provide scholarly and analytical input while political organizations can provide relevance for policy-making process.

1. The Programme in Arms Control, Disarmament, and International Security (ACDIS), University of Illinois-Urbana, has been running a South Asian Security and Arms Con-

trol Training Project since 1978. ACDIS brings South Asian strategists, scholars, and journalists to Urbana for one semester or one academic year to work on arms control-related projects or otherwise enhance their skills and knowledge. Over 60 individuals have been resident in Urbana, and a reunion-conference was held in Kathmandu in 1992, resulting in a book on South Asian security in the post-Cold War period.

2. The Stimson Centre, Washington DC, has, for the past three years, had a special sub-programme for the training of South Asians in current developments in confidence-building measures.

3. India-Pakistan Neemrana Initiative on regional security issues began in 1992 by the U.S. Information Service (USIS). Now funded by private sources, it involves 16 Indians and Pakistanis meeting thrice a year. The chair is an American (Dr Paul Kreisberg). So far, there is little agreement on specific subjects but jointly written papers may soon be forthcoming.

4. The U.S. Information Agency has organized a series of WORLDNET (closed-circuit television) broadcasts linking Indian, Pakistani, and American experts in discussions of regional issues. These, and Neemrana, had their origins in a series of 1990-'91 regional "Dartmouth" seminars organized by Mr Harold Saunders, a former U.S. government official closely associated with the Middle East peace process in several administrations.

5. The O.P. Shah Initiatives coordinated by Mr Shah, a Calcutta-based chartered accountant, include India-Pakistan meetings using contributions by participants who range across the political and social spectrum. Each meeting (held so far both in India and Pakistan) features one or more public sessions and extended private or closed sessions.

6. The Punjab Haryana Delhi Chamber of Commerce (from offices located just outside Delhi) has initiated a dialogue among small-scale businessmen in India and Pakistan. It

also publishes a regular comprehensive newsletter on India-Pakistan business prospects.

7. The Regional Policy Dialogue brings together representatives from South Asia's leading policy study centres for discussions on contemporary policy issues. Members typically are retired civil servants, journalists, and senior academics. The Centre for Policy Research (CPR), New Delhi, is the chief organizer.

8. The Regional Centre for Strategic Studies (RCSS) in Colombo, evolved as a result of discussions among regional scholars, will assist regional centres in networking with each other. RCSS is located in the Bandaranaike Centre, Sri Lanka. RCSS will sponsor collaborative research projects. A directory of nearly 600 individuals and centres with an interest in South Asian security and strategic issues has been published.

9. The South Asian Summer School in Arms Control was conceived by Dr. George Perkovich. This is an annual summer school for younger South Asian (and Chinese) journalists, officials, and scholars (about 25-30 participants, six to eight international faculty). The first School was held in 1993 at Bhurban, Pakistan, a hill-station above Islamabad. The second session was held in May 1994, also in Pakistan and the third in India. The goals are to transfer state-of-the-art knowledge about arms control verification, and conflict resolution, and to create a network of younger scholars that transcends regional borders. Faculty include South Asian, Chinese, and Western experts.

10. India-China Dialogues have been organized by various institutes. In recent years at least five Chinese groups have been to India to study Indian economic, commercial, administrative systems. A few Indian delegations have visited Chinese strategic centres.

11. U.S.-Indian Strategic Talks. Three years ago the National Defense University (NDU), Washington, D.C., with the encouragement of the Department of Defense, began a series of "strategic dialogues" between Indian and Ameri-

can strategists. The Indian co-sponsor has been the Institute for Defense Studies and Analysis, New Delhi. The last dialogue was held in early 1996. The dialogue has resulted in a few books and has often been less notable for in-conference discussions than for serving as the venue for informal talks between participants and officials in out-of-conference settings.

12. U.S.-Pakistan Dialogues. NDU has organized a joint seminar with Institute for Strategic Studies, Islamabad, in the United States. This is a revival of several quasi-official academic dialogues held between Pakistanis and Americans in the 1980s. There is some discussion of combining this with a revived U.S-India dialogue in a three-way meeting.

13. The Friedrich Ebert Stiftung, Germany, had sponsored a working group on regional economic cooperation since 1990 that examined political conflict and the benefits of cooperation. It organized a large conference to release its sectoral studies in May 1994. Several publications on the subject have come out since then.

14. The United Nations Regional Centre for Peace and Disarmament in Asia and the Pacific was established in 1988 as part of the UN effort to create regional disarmament centres. It organizes an annual conference in Kathmandu on Asian disarmament issues and has sponsored conferences on regional disarmament, confidence-building, and related subjects in Japan.

15. Chinese funding to Sri Lanka and Nepal for setting up very substantial conference centres in Colombo and Kathmandu. These have extensive facilities for international conferences. The Colombo centre (Bandaranaike Memorial International Conference Hall—BMICH) also houses the Bandaranaike Centre for International Studies (BCIS).

16. TOUCH (The Organization for Universal Communal Harmony) is a Chicago-based inter-community organization devoted to promoting "inter-communal peace and harmony" in South Asia. Its founder-director, Dr Nazar Hayat Tiwana,

has sponsored a number of programmes in India, but the group also has strong contacts in Pakistan (Dr Tiwana's father was the head of the pre-partition Unionist Party in undivided Punjab).

17. The Swedes, the Germans, and the Finns each fund one or more South Asian scholars each year to study arms control in their respective countries. The Japanese are building expertise and have recently held the annual South Asian conferences at the Japan Institute for International Affairs, Tokyo, with regional invitees from South Asia.

18. The Council on Foreign Relations, New York, has completed a study of U.S.-South Asian relations. Key members include former Ambassadors Shirin Tahir-Kheli and Richard Murphy.

19. South Asia Co-ordination Committee for Multinational Enterprise Trade Unions has membership in 20 multinational corporations in South Asia. The committee promotes cooperation among members.

20. Kashmir Humanitarian Initiative is the first ever CBM between people of Kashmir and the rest of India. A factfinding mission of International Centre for Peace Initiatives visited Srinagar in June 1995 and decided to launch health care and employment generation projects on the ground with the cooperation of Kashmiri community groups and Bombay NGOs. Militant leaders have assured safety of the projects. The ICPI is also organizing seminars on the political dimension of the Kashmir issue involving top militant leaders and Indian political leaders.

21. India-Bangladesh Dialogue is a programme of regular exchange of views between politicians and scholars on trade, transit, water and refugees. A project of Centre for Policy Research, New Delhi, and Centre for Policy Dialogue, Dhaka.

22. South Asian Women Leaders for Peace and Cooperation: Friedrich Ebert Foundation is planning to bring together women political leaders, especially members of parliament, from the seven SAARC member countries—with a

view to developing the female perspective on peace and cooperation and contribute it to the region's policy agenda. A meeting was held in New Delhi in 1995.

23. Pakistan-India People's Forum is a group of NGO representatives from the two countries meeting in Lahore and New Delhi alternately to advocate diversion of funds from military to rural development. Two meetings of the forum have been held in New Delhi and Lahore. Over 200 people participated in the last meeting in November 1995. Dr Mubashir Hassan, Pakistan's former finance minister, is the project coordinator.

24. South Asia Media Association is lobbying for the inclusion of bilateral conflict resolution in the framework of SAARC. SAMA held a seminar in Islamabad, a week before the New Delhi SAARC Summit in 1995, to urge the heads of government to consider its proposition.

25. Coalition for Action on South Asian Cooperation (CASAC) was established in May 1995 to mobilize individuals and NGOs to promote regional cooperation. Several seminars and publications are planned for 1996/97. Mr K.K. Bhargava, former secretary-general of SAARC, is the convener.

10

Proposal for South Asian Parliament

By Javed Jabbar

SINCE the inception of SAARC in Dhaka, Bangladesh, in December 1985, the region has been marked by two conflicting trends. One trend is the movement towards multi-party democratic systems in each of the seven countries, culminating in a majority of them in the formation of representative institutions. Though there are ample grounds to question the authenticity of the electoral process in some cases, the region-wide preference for a democratic and political approach to development is fairly clear and unambiguous, despite the difficulties being faced in the operation of the democratic system.

At the same time, a second trend has become pronounced in the past few years in the region. This is the heightening of tension and conflict, both between the nation-states of South Asia and ethnic or religious polarization within nation-states.

In what constitutes one of the most important regions of the world, representing one-fifth of humanity, there is no single mechanism that provides an opportunity for these two trends to be simultaneously reflected, analyzed and contained.

Under the current democratic freedom being witnessed by the nations of South Asia, the political leaders shoot and shout their rhetoric regarding relations with other States in a kind of vacuum chamber because the fora in which the invective, or the goodwill, as the case may be, are expressed, are strictly domestic.

If nothing else, a regional Parliament would serve as a useful place to let off steam where representatives could vent all their contrasting, conflicting viewpoints. Through the process of listening directly to each other about what they thought of each other without the restrictions that government-to-government dialogue requires, the peoples' representatives would be able to move closer towards a commonality of positions on vital issues, building on the strengths that they share rather than concentrating on the divisive elements alone.

Within the larger South Asian people's community setting, solutions to historic and difficult problems that have bedevilled bilateral relations between two neighbours could also be gainfully pursued.

One significant and immediate benefit would surely be an improved environment for minorities because the dynamics of dialogue between political parties that have a communal dimension with national frontiers temporarily removed are bound to increase tolerance and reduce religious animosities.

For the foreseeable future, the exclusive function of a Regional Parliament would be to serve as a forum for conflict-resolution on a mass level, as a peace-making forum on the political level, with no legislative duties except those that can promote solutions to disputes. Each country of South Asia would preserve its internal legislative sovereignty while participating in the South Asian Parliament. If official participation is initially difficult, then Parliament could assemble regularly on a non-official, people-to-people basis.

Existing modes of contact between the seven nations on a regional basis as provided by the SAARC mechanisms are either too sectoral and fragmented as in the case of cooperation in telecommunications and agricultural research or too rigid and protocolized as in the case of the summit-level meetings where the absence of a single Head of State or Government can be used as a device to torpedo the whole summit itself.

Sectoral cooperation is necessary and useful, serving as slow, step-by-step approach towards cooperation between nations. But it is confined to specialized and professional interaction rather than contact at the popular level which is critical to the objective of strengthening friendship amongst South Asian nations.

The pressing urgency of the problems faced by the people of South Asia, the abiding agony of acute poverty, illiteracy, ill-health, and deprivation cannot afford the luxury of a cautious and evolutionary approach to the desirable condition of regional peace and stability in which condition alone these basic problems can be effectively tackled.

For over 40 years this conventional and stereotypical evolutionary approach has been followed with predictably marginal progress. In an age when advancement of human knowledge is proceeding at a blistering pace, the rate of movement in South Asia towards regional cooperation is ponderous and plodding, out of step with the needs of the people and out of synch with the rest of the world.

While in other parts of the planet, vast state structures are collapsing and are being re-organized, where whole ideologies are being discarded or are being revamped, where new nation-states are emerging, old wounds continue to fester in South Asia; sometimes reopening at every touch of the expired medicines that continue to be applied.

The nature of inter-governmental relations in the region on a multilateral as well as a bilateral basis moves from one extreme of a fixed and static position to the other extreme of a see-saw in which meetings between government leaders produce brief promises of progress only to revert quickly to mutual suspicion and hostility.

There is thus a distinct need for a new initiative that breaks with the inhibiting patterns of the past to define new directions for dialogue and discussion, for conversation and communication between the people who represent the broad range of public opinion in the region.

Governments tend almost exclusively to represent single political parties or, in some cases, coalitions which nevertheless still represent a limited segment of the total population. In the multi-party parliamentary systems that substantively characterize at least five of the seven South Asian nations (with the Maldives and Bhutan being the exceptions) and these representing the overwhelming bulk of the region's population of one billion people, it is imperative to create a system by which the major political parties of all seven nations are able to engage in regular, in-depth, direct communication with each other.

By bringing together major political parties from each country into contact with the principal political forces of neighbouring countries, parliament would enable parties that are traditional adversaries within their own countries and which prevent each other from taking an innovative approach to unresolved problems in the region, to forge a consensus within each country regarding new paths to peace.

When a political party establishes a government it also inherits a set of enduring official assumptions and perceptions on important policy issues concerning relations with other nations in the region. Some of these inherited perceptions are valid but in the absence of a pluralist political perspective which can only be provided by reference to the breadth of political opinion prevailing in a given country and across the region, the entrenched establishment view of peace and conflict in South Asia tends to determine the patterns of inter-state relations even after a new government, or governments, take office.

A permanent parliament of South Asia would thus provide the large canvas that the scale of the region deserves. This would be a canvas upon which a transcending vision of peace and unity could be outlined and then filled in with hues and shades even when governments, as they come and go, would initially tend to stick to the tones that they have long used.

Gradually, cumulatively, over a period of years and decades, but sooner than later, the existence of a parliamentary framework on a South Asian basis would help erode the obstacles of suspicion and hate that have so far shaped the course of relations.

The composition of a South Asian parliament could be determined by a combination of some, or all, of the following elements.

First, all political parties of a country that have polled at least 10 per cent of the national vote in the previous one or two general elections would be entitled to nominate say, five representatives each to the South Asian Parliament.

Then, assuming that from each of the larger population South Asian countries (Pakistan, India, Bangladesh, Sri Lanka and Nepal) we could obtain 20 representatives from 4 leading political parties or coalitions of each country we would get a total of about 100 representatives. From the two South Asian countries i.e., Bhutan and Maldives which have extremely small populations and do not have vigorous multi-party systems, on the principle of equity, we could also obtain 20 representatives chosen by nomination or consensus within their respective countries to provide an initial number of a hundred and forty individuals.

Secondly, in order to provide the valuable resource of specialized knowledge and experience each country could nominate five technocrats in fields such as economics, education, health, defence and development.

Thirdly, all former Heads of State and Heads of Government who are able to participate should be entitled to participate in the deliberations of a South Asian Parliament so that the assembly benefits from their specific experience and insights.

Fourthly, to prevent the membership of a South Asian Parliament from being subject to unduly frequent changes caused by the holding of unscheduled elections or the ouster of governments within on-going legislatures, a percentage of the seats of the regional parliament could be allocated to political parties and representative organizations for a fixed term on the basis of their share of the vote over the past two or three elections while the remaining seats of the parliament could be directly determined by the results of each election in the nations of the region.

In its initial formative phase, during which its potential and its actual performance can be studied, such a parliament could comprise about 250 to 300 people, representing virtually the entire range of political and public opinion throughout South Asia while at the same time benefitting from the expert opinion of professionals and of the past official leadership.

To avoid exposing the tender sapling of regional democracy to bilateral conflict, the venue for the meetings of the South Asian Parliament during the first five years—till the present degree of virtually frozen relations is thawed out a little—should be the capital of a country that is not part of the over-heated bilateral grid of Pakistan-India, Sri Lanka-India or India-Bangladesh relations. Kathmandu thus suggests itself as the ideal venue for this Assembly.

One essential step forward towards a Parliament of South Asia is a coming together for a few days of the leadership of the major political parties of South Asia: a kind of South Asian political parties conference which could examine the feasibility of this proposal on a face-to-face basis and formalize a mechanism to obtain both governmental endorsement as well as wider non-governmental support. In the year ahead, it is intended to create the organizational basis for such a conference with equal participation from public figures of all seven nations.

The real scope and complexity of the linkages between the peoples of the seven South Asian nations containing, in turn, within themselves, a very large number of sub-nationalities and communities with a spectacular variety of languages, cultures, races and faiths, deserves a forum of direct people-to-people communication that encompasses, but does not exclusively consist of, government-to-government relations.

A regional parliament would provide a permanent and comprehensive framework for a continuous exchange of facts and opinions between the elected and political representatives of the people within which changes of governments and shifts of policies could occur without disrupting the enduring process of communication.

Selected Bibliography

1. The American Academy of Political and Social Science. *Peace studies: past and future*. Special editor: George A. Lopez. Sage, 1989. 180p.
2. Bok, Sissela. *A Strategy for peace: human values and the threat of war*. Pantheon Books, 1989. 202p.
3. Center for the Study of Foreign Affairs. *National negotiating styles*. Edited by Hans Binnendijk. Foreign Service Institute, U.S. Department of State, April 1987.
4. Cohen, Raymond. *Threat perception in international crisis*. University of Wisconsin Press, 1979. 229p.
5. Dunlop, John Thomas. *Dispute resolution: negotiation and consensus building*. Auburn House Pub. Co., 1984. 296p.
6. Fisher, Roger. *Getting to yes: negotiating agreement without giving in*. Roger Fisher and William Ury with Bruce Patton, editor. Penguin Books, 1983, 1981. 161p.
7. *The Future conflict*. Edited by John J. McIntyre. National Defense University Press; USGPO, 1979. 186p.
8. *A Game for high stakes: lessons learned in negotiating with the Soviet Union*. Edited by Leon Sloss and M. Scott Davis. Ballinger Pub. Co., 1986. 184p.
9. Habeeb, William Mark. *Power and tactics in international negotiation: how weak nations bargain with strong nations*. Johns Hopkins University Press, 1988. 168p.
10. *Handbook of political conflict: theory and research*. Edited

by Ted Robert Gurr. Free Press, 1980. 566p.

11. *International mediation in theory and practice.* Saadia Touval and I. William Zartman, editors. Westview Press with the Foreign Policy Institute, School of Advanced International Studies, the Johns Hopkins University Press, 1985. 274p.

12. Mitchell, Christopher Roger. *The Structure of international conflict.* St Martin's Press, 1981. 355p.

13. Pneuman, Roy W. *Managing conflict: a complete process-centered handbook.* Roy W. Pneuman and Margaret E. Bruehl. Prentice-Hall, 1982. 128p.

14. Snyder, Glenn Herald. *Conflict among nations: bargaining, decision making, and system structure in international crisis.* Glenn H. Snyder and Paul Diesing. Princeton University Press, 1977. 578p.

15. Wehr, Paul. *Conflict regulation.* Foreword by Kenneth E. Boulding, Westview Press, 1979. 245p.

16. Zartman, I. William. *The Practical negotiator.* I. William Zartman and Maureen R. Berman. Yale University Press, 1982. 250p.

17. The American Academy of Political and Social Science. *Resolving regional conflicts: international perspectives.* Special editor: I. William Zartman. Sage Publications, 1991. 230p.

18. Burton, John Wear. *Conflict: practices in management, settlement and resolution.* John Burton and Frank Dukes. St Martin's Press, 1990. 230p.

19. Haass, Richard. *Conflicts unending: the United States and regional disputes.* Richard N. Haass. Yale University Press, 1990. 172p.

20. *International negotiation: analysis, approaches, issues.* Victor A. Kremenyuk, editor. Jossey-Bass Publishers, 1991. 486p.

21. Saunders, Harold H. *The Other Walls: The Arab-Israeli Peace Process in Global Perspective.* Affiliated East-West Press Pvt Ltd, 1992.

22. Shri Prakash. *Causes of Conflicts in the Third World During the Post-Cold War Phase.* Jamia Millia Islamia, 1993.

23. Fisher, Roger. *Beyond Machiavelli: Tools for Coping with*

Conflict. Roger Fisher, Elizabeth Kopelman and Andrea Kupfer Schneider. Harvard University Press, 1994.

24. Burton, John. *Conflict: Readings in Management and Resolution*. John Burton and Frank Dukes. St Martin's Press, 1990.

25. Krepon, Michael. *A Handbook of Confidence building Measures for Regional Security* (2nd Edition). The Henry L. Stimson Center, 1995.

26. Sandole, Dennis J.D. *Conflict Resolution Theory and Practice*. Edited by Dennis J.D. Sandole and Hugo van der Merwe. Manchester University Press.

27. Worchel, S. *Conflict Between People and Groups*. Edited by S. Worchel and J. Simpson, Nelson Hall. 1993.

28. Workshop material prepared for various workshops by International Peace Academy, New York
Parliamentarians for Global Action, New York
Conflict Management Group at Harvard, Cambridge

Relevant publications by the staff of the International Centre for Peace Initiatives

1. *The New World Order* (hard cover), pp 214, New Delhi: Konark, 1991.

2. *Abolishing Nuclear Weapons: Rajiv Gandhi Plan Revisited*, Urbana: ACDIS, University of Illinois, 1994.

3. *Track Two Diplomacy in South Asia*, Urbana: ACDIS, University of Illinois, 1994 (1st ed), 1995 (2nd ed).

4. Agenda for Peace, *Peace Initiatives*, Vol. 1, No. 1, 1995.

5. Kashmir Fact-finding Mission Report, *Peace Initiatives*, Vol. 1, No. 2, 1995.

6. Political Leaders and Track Two Diplomacy in South Asia, *Peace Initiatives*, Vol. 1, No. 3, 1995.

7. *South Asian Drama: Travails of Misgovernance* (hard cover), pp 388, New Delhi: Konark, 1996

For More Information

Mr Sundeep Waslekar
Director
International Centre for Peace Initiatives
B-704 Montana, Lokhandwala Complex
Andheri West, Bombay 400 053
India
Tel: 91-22-6265672 / Fax: 91-22-6318260

The International Centre for Peace Initiatives was established in Bombay, India, in 1990 to conceptualize, develop and promote innovative approaches to peace at global, regional and national levels.

The Centre addresses long-term needs of peace since peace has no finishing line. It acts as a catalyst in partnership with leading institutions. It sees its role as a social entrepreneur on the leading edge of the world's and India's public policy agenda.

In its five years of existence, the Centre has successfully completed pioneering projects involving the participation of Nobel laureates, serving and former heads of government, and distinguished scholars from all parts of the world.

In the early 1990s the Centre had focussed on advocating a cooperative security regime free of nuclear weapons. Since 1994 the Centre is engaged in various processes of conflict resolution in South Asia. It aims at involving political leaders in peace-making. It has special interest in the Kashmir conflict and India-Pakistan relations.

In view of India's new economic policies and the increasingly important role of business in the society, the Centre has launched an initiative for facilitating a constructive role of the Indian business in developing a strategic vision for a prosperous and internally secure India by 2022 AD.

The Centre also publishes a bi-monthly journal, undertakes contract research on regional security and cooperation issues and offers exposure programmes for students.